Pies and Mini Pies

Join the Mini Pie Explosion

Bonnie Scott

BONNIE SCOTT

Copyright © 2012 Bonnie Scott

All rights reserved.

ISBN-13: 978-1480285354

PIES AND MINI PIES: JOIN THE MINI PIE EXPLOSION

THE ANATOMY OF A MINI PIE	11
FRUIT PIES	**16**
How Much Fruit To Use For A Nine Inch Pie	16
Prevent Runny Pie Filling	17
Creamy Peach Pie	18
Creamy Peach Mini Pies	19
Sugarless Apple Pie	20
Sugarless Apple Mini Pies	21
Pineapple Pie	22
Pineapple Mini Pies	23
Glazed Strawberry Pie	24
Quick Fried Pies	25
Blueberry Pie	26
Blueberry Mini Pies	27
Old Fashioned Apple Pie	28
Old Fashioned Apple Mini Pies	29
Ginger Fruit Pie	31
Magic Blackberry Pie	32
Swedish Apple Pie	33
Perfect Cherry Pie	34
Perfect Cherry Mini Pies	35
Cranberry Apple Pie	36
Cranberry Apple Mini Pies	37
Apple Crumb Pie	38
Apple Crumb Mini Pies	39
Texas Grapefruit Pie	40
Texas Grapefruit Mini Pies	41
Japanese Fruit Pie	42
Japanese Fruit Mini Pies	43
Blueberry Peach Pie	44
Blueberry Peach Mini Pies	45
Backyard Pie	46
Backyard Mini Pies	47
Glaze for Fresh Fruit Pies	48

CUSTARD PIES   50

Custard Pie Tips	50
Double Layer Pumpkin Pie	**51**
Coconut Custard Pie	**52**
Coconut Custard Mini Pies	53
Old Dutch Shoo-Fly Pie	**54**
Plum Custard Pie	**55**
Pecan Pie	**56**
Pecan Mini Pies	57
Black Raspberry Custard Pie	**58**
Black Raspberry Custard Mini Pies	59
Easy Pumpkin Pie	**60**
Easy Pumpkin Mini Pies	61
Ultimate Caramel Chocolate Pecan Pie	**62**
Ultimate Caramel Chocolate Pecan Mini Pies	63
Custard Pie	**64**
Custard Mini Pies	65
Fudge Pecan Pie	**66**
Fudge Pecan Mini Pies	67
Graham Cracker Pie	**68**
Sour Cream and Blueberry Pie	**69**
Egg Custard Pie	**70**
Egg Custard Mini Pies	71
Mock Mincemeat Pie	**72**
Mock Mincemeat Mini Pies	73

CREAM PIES   75

Manse Style Blueberry Cream Pie	**76**
Manse Style Blueberry Mini Pies	77
Magic Lemon Cream Pie	**78**
Raspberry Meringue Pie	**79**
Chocolate Angel Strata Pie	**80**
Five Layer Banana Cream Pie	**82**
Five Layer Banana Cream Mini Pies	83
Butterscotch Cream Pie	**84**
Butterscotch Cream Mini Pies	85
Cherry Cream Pie	**86**

CHERRY CREAM MINI PIES — 87
BANANA CREAM PIE — **88**
BANANA CREAM MINI PIES — 89
WHITE CHOCOLATE COCO CREAM PIE — **90**
LEMON-BLUEBERRY CREAM PIE — **91**
FROZEN PEACH CREAM PIE — **92**
FROZEN PEACH CREAM MINI PIES — 93
EASY PINEAPPLE CREAM PIE — **94**
EASY PINEAPPLE CREAM MINI PIES — 95
APPLE CREAM PIE — **96**
APPLE CREAM MINI PIES — 97

REFRIGERATED PIES — 99

FRENCH CHERRY PIE — **100**
FRENCH CHERRY MINI PIES — 101
CHOCOLATE TURTLE PIE — **102**
CHEESECAKE PIE — **103**
CHOCOLATE NUT FLUFF PIE — **104**
CHOCOLATE NUT FLUFF MINI PIES — 105
FROZEN LEMON PIE — **106**
WAIKKI PIE — **107**
FRENCH SILK CHOCOLATE PIE — **108**
FRENCH SILK CHOCOLATE MINI PIES — 109
HERSHEY BAR PIE — **110**
HERSHEY BAR MINI PIES — 111
MILE HIGH PIE — **112**
OREO COOKIE PIE — **113**
DAIQUIRI PIE — **114**
DAIQUIRI MINI PIES — 115
PINEAPPLE JELLO PIE — **116**
PINEAPPLE JELLO MINI PIES — 117
NEW ENGLAND BLUEBERRY PIE — **118**
NEW ENGLAND BLUEBERRY MINI PIES — 119
HEAVENLY YOGURT PIE — **120**
HEAVENLY YOGURT MINI PIES — 121
MARVELOUS MOCHA PIE — **122**
KEY LIME PIE — **123**
CHERRY CHEESE PIE — **124**

Pies and Mini Pies

You'll soon be baking pies with confidence with these 100 great pie and mini pie recipes. From homey fruit pies, custard and cream pies to pies with unusual ingredients, there are pies for every occasion. You'll find chapters for tarts and toppings, crusts and refrigerated pies. You will also find great hints and tips for preparing a perfect pie that even your grandmother would be proud to serve.

Whether you're a seasoned pro or a beginning baker, you'll find recipes your family will be asking for again and again. You'll also learn how to create mini pies from your standard pie recipes. Mini pies are a great way to serve a crowd and are perfect gifts for the holidays.

Mini Pies

Join the mini pie explosion! Bite size mini pies are all the rage. The teeny tiny pies are so easy to eat and portion control is built in. These little baked goods are so cute displayed in cupcake racks or put together into a shape like a Christmas tree for holiday parties. They make perfect party hors-d'oeuvres since they are finger food. And they are fun to make and can be made in advance of your get together.

In this recipe book, you'll learn how to make two sizes of mini pies from regular pie recipes. One mini pie is made using a regular muffin/cupcake tin (2 3/4"). The second itty bitty pie is made using a mini muffin pan which will make 1 3/4" mini pies.

Not every recipe in this book has a mini pie variation but most do. If you would like to try a mini pie and there is no mini pie recipe for that particular recipe, just find a similar one that does have the mini pie recipe and adjust it.

REMOVING THE PIES - Be sure your mini pie pans are non-stick for ease of removal. Otherwise the fragile tiny pie may break into pieces. Let the mini pie cool in the pan before attempting to remove it. Spraying the muffin cup with Pam first also helps in removal.

Another tip is to cut strips of parchment paper to use as handles for removing the pies. Lay a strip of parchment paper down in each mini muffin cup or muffin cup with about an inch sticking above the muffin cup on each end. Then add the pie crust. Mini pies will lift right out with their handles when they are finished baking.

BAKING TEMPERATURE AND TIME – Using small mini muffin pans or regular muffin pans will cause your pies to cook a bit quicker than a large pie. I recommend you turn the oven temperature to 350 or 375 degrees F, cook the pies for 15 to 20 minutes and if they need more time, check them every 5 minutes so they don't overcook.

If the mini pie has a top crust and it is browning too quickly, just like with a regular size pie, you can use tin foil around the edges of the mini or just cover the whole pan lightly with tin foil.

AMOUNT OF FILLING – If you fill the muffin cups too full of a juicy filling, like blueberry pie filling, the filling may rise and kind of explode onto your pan, especially if you have a top crust on it. The juicy filling will actually lift up the top crust so it can ooze out the sides. So I recommend testing a few and try filling the muffin cups 2/3's or 3/4's full of pie filling.

PIE CRUST – It's easy to use a pie crust recipe or refrigerated pre-made pie crusts for the mini pies. Just use a cup or bowl that is 3" to 4" in circumference, depending on your mini muffin pan, cut circles from the dough and press them into the muffin cup.

For the tiny mini muffin pans, it works great to make a pie crust recipe, then roll the pastry into balls and press the balls into the bottom and up sides of muffin cups. The flour based recipes make a better mini pie crust, just because the crust can be made thinner than is possible with the graham cracker crusts. The pastry recipe for the Mississippi Mud Pie would be a nice substitute for a graham cracker crust.

A cute way to decorate your tiny pies is to use teeny cookie cutters to cut out shapes in the dough and place on top. Use Christmas shapes for the holidays, hearts for Valentine's Day and pumpkins for Halloween.

The Anatomy of a Mini Pie

This is a step by step walk through of preparing the Mississippi Mud Mini Pie, found in the refrigerated pie section of this book, using a non-stick mini muffin pan.

First, spray the non-stick mini muffin pan with Pam and add 5 to 6 inch strips of parchment paper in each cup. The paper will stick to the Pam and stay in place. The parchment paper will act as handles and allow lifting the tiny pies out in one piece.

Add refrigerated whipped topping on top and some nuts or chocolate sprinkles. Refrigerate for 3 hours, then remove the teeny pies using the parchment paper handles.

FRUIT PIES

Fruit Pies

Fresh summer fruits and berries are the stars of these delicious desserts. Whether you're making a classic apple pie, a creamy peach pie or baking up a medley of your favorite berries, you'll find recipes that take full advantage of the season's harvest.

No fresh fruit on hand? No problem. There are several recipes that use canned fruit and pie fillings for a tasty treat any time of the year. You'll even find a recipe for fried pie made with dried fruit for a country taste that takes you back to the days of the pioneers.

How Much Fruit To Use For A Nine Inch Pie

These are general approximations:

Rhubarb - Five to six cups

Apple - Six to eight cups

Apples shrink when cooking, so use a generous, heaping pile.

Cherry - Six cups

Apricot - Five to six cups

Raspberry - Six cups

Blueberry - Six cups

*Peach - Five to six cups

Blackberry - Six cups

Strawberry - Six cups

*Peaches are very juicy. You may wish to sprinkle the slices with a little sugar, toss to coat and drain in a colander for 15 minutes before adding to your crust. This removes some of the liquid to help keep the pie from being runny.

Prevent Runny Pie Filling

Often the cause of runny pie filling is inadequate baking time. Try baking your pie 5 to 10 minutes longer.

If that doesn't work, sprinkle a spoon of tapioca over the filling before baking. You can also use one tablespoon of tapioca powder per one cup of liquid. Combine the the powder with your ingredients and simmer for 15 minutes.

Mix corn starch with your recipe in a ratio of one tablespoon cornstarch per one and one half cups of liquid. This makes a nice, clear thickener.

Sugarless Apple Pie

2 unbaked pie crusts
2 teaspoons cornstarch
1 12 ounce can apple juice concentrate
4 cups apples, peeled and sliced
1 teaspoon cinnamon
1 teaspoon margarine

Mix cornstarch and apple juice concentrate in pan. Cook and stir until it begins to clear. Stir in apples and cinnamon. Pour into pie crust and top with margarine. Lay top crust over filling. Bake at 350 degrees F for 35 to 45 minutes.

Sugarless Apple Mini Pies

** Cut the apples into smaller bite-size pieces for mini pies.
** Use 2 9" crusts for 12 muffin cups or 24 mini muffin cups.

Spray muffin pans with Pam. Add a strip of parchment paper to each muffin cup to use as handles for removing the tiny pies easily. Fill with pie crust as directed below, depending on your mini pie size.

Make the Sugarless Apple Pie filling according to this recipe. Only fill muffin cups 3/4 full with pie filling. TOPS - Add lattice pastry strips, use tiny cookie cutters in pastry, top with pie crust (slit top for venting) or just leave the top open. Pinch the crusts together if topping with pie crust.

Mini pies bake a little faster than regular pies. Cook the mini apple pies for about 15 to 20 minutes at 350 or 375 degrees F. If additional cooking time is needed, check the pies frequently until the crust is golden. Cool in pan.

muffin pan recipe

Muffin/Cupcake Pan: 2-3/4" mini pies

Pie crust: Cut 3-1/2" or 4" circles with a biscuit cutter or use a bowl to cut the circle. Shape the pie crust into each muffin cup.

mini muffin pan recipe

Mini Muffin Pan: 1-3/4" mini pies

Pie Crust: Make your favorite pie crust recipe. Roll the dough into 24 balls about 1" in diameter. Press the balls into the bottom and up sides of muffin cups.

Refrigerated Pie Crust: Cut 3" circles with a cookie cutter and shape into each muffin cup.

Pineapple Pie

1 unbaked pie shell
1 can crushed pineapple
1/2 to 3/4 cup sugar
3 tablespoons cornstarch
3 egg yolks – 3 egg whites

Whip egg whites until stiff and fold into mixture of pineapple, sugar, cornstarch and yolks. Pour into unbaked pie shell and bake 30 minutes at 425 degrees F.

Pineapple Mini Pies

** Use 2 9" crusts for 12 muffin cups or 24 mini muffin cups.

Spray muffin pans with Pam. Add a strip of parchment paper to the muffin cup to use as handles for removing the pie easily. Fill with pie crust as directed below, depending on your mini pie size.

Make the Pineapple Pie filling according to this recipe. Only fill muffin cups 3/4 full with pie filling. TOPS - Add lattice pastry strips, use tiny cookie cutters in pastry, top with pie crust (slit top for venting) or just leave the top open. Pinch the crusts together if topping with pie crust.

Mini pies bake a little faster than regular pies. Cook the pineapple pies for about 15 to 20 minutes at 350 or 375 degrees F. If additional cooking time is needed, check the pies frequently until the crust is golden. Cool in pan.

muffin pan recipe

Muffin/Cupcake Pan: 2-3/4" mini pies

Pie crust: Cut 3-1/2" or 4" circles with a biscuit cutter or use a bowl to cut the circle. Shape the pie crust into each muffin cup.

mini muffin pan recipe

Mini Muffin Pan: 1-3/4" mini pies

Pie Crust: Make your favorite pie crust recipe. Roll the dough into 24 balls about 1" in diameter. Press the balls into the bottom and up sides of muffin cups.

Refrigerated Pie Crust: Cut 3" circles with a cookie cutter and shape into each muffin cup.

Glazed Strawberry Pie

1 baked pie shell
1 quart strawberries washed and stemmed
1 cup sugar
1/2 cup water
1/4 cup cornstarch
3/4 cup cold water
1/8 teaspoon salt
1 tablespoon lemon juice
Few drops red food coloring
1 baked pastry pie shell

Bring sugar and 1/2 cup water to boiling. Dissolve cornstarch in 3/4 cup cold water. Add to sugar syrup mixture. Cook about 10 minutes over low heat or until clear. Blend in salt, lemon juice and food coloring. Pour glaze over strawberries and mix gently. Put mixture in baked pie shell.

Quick Fried Pies

1 can flaky buttermilk biscuits
1 lb. dried fruit (your choice)
1/2 cup sugar
1 cup powdered sugar
3 teaspoons of cinnamon
2 heaping tablespoons vegetable shortening

Roll each biscuit until it is the size of a small plate. Cook the dried fruit with a little sugar until tender. Let cool. Then spoon a full teaspoon of the cooked fruit into the center of each flattened biscuit. Fold over (making a half-moon). Tuck the edges in and mash them with the tines of a fork. Repeat with next biscuit. Lay each pie on a flat sheet until all the biscuits have been used.

Then in a skillet with the vegetable shortening brought to medium heat (not too hot), fry the pies on both sides. Warning: The pies are easily burned; so watch them every moment.

Make a glaze, using a mixture of powdered sugar, cinnamon and water and brush over the pies before they cool.

Blueberry Pie

1 baked 9" pie shell
1 large cream cheese
1 cup confectioner's sugar
1 package Dream Whip®
1/2 cup milk
1 teaspoon vanilla
Can of blueberry pie filling

Mix cream cheese with sugar. Add Dream Whip, milk and vanilla. Put in pie shell. Pour berries over mixture.

PIES AND MINI PIES: JOIN THE MINI PIE EXPLOSION

Blueberry Mini Pies

** Use 2 9" crusts for 12 muffin cups or 24 mini muffin cups.
** Refrigerator pie crusts may be used.
** Add filling from blueberry recipe after baking and cooling the mini pie crusts.

Spray muffin pans with Pam. Add a strip of parchment paper to the muffin cup to use as handles for removing the tiny pies easily. Fill muffin cups with pastry as directed below, depending on your mini pie size.

muffin pan recipe

Muffin/Cupcake Pan: 2-3/4" mini pies

Pie crust: Cut 3-1/2" or 4" circles with a biscuit cutter or use a bowl to cut the circle. Shape the pie crust into each regular size muffin cup. Bake at 450 degrees F for 8 to 10 minutes or until lightly browned.

mini muffin pan recipe

Mini Muffin Pan: 1-3/4" mini pies

Pie Crust: Make your favorite pie crust recipe. Roll the dough into 24 balls about 1" in diameter. Press the balls into the bottom and up sides of muffin cups. Bake at 400 degrees F 6 to 8 minutes or until lightly browned.

Refrigerated Pie Crust: Cut 3" circles using a round cutter and shape into each mini muffin cup or roll the dough into 24 balls about 1" in diameter. Press the balls into the bottom and up sides of mini muffin cups. Bake at 400 degrees F 6 to 8 minutes or until lightly browned.

Old Fashioned Apple Pie

Pie Crust:

2 cups flour
2/3 cup shortening
3 tablespoons water
1 teaspoon salt

Blend flour, salt and shortening with pastry blender, then reserve 1/4 cup of mixture and set aside for later.

Filling:

6 apples – pare, core and slice
3/4 cup sugar
1/4 teaspoon salt
1 teaspoon cinnamon
1 tablespoon butter

Roll out bottom crust and put in pie pan. Put in apples and cover with sugar, salt and cinnamon. Dot with butter. Roll out top crust and cover pie. Take reserved mixture and add 2 teaspoons sugar. Mix and sprinkle over pie before baking at 350 degrees F for one hour.

PIES AND MINI PIES: JOIN THE MINI PIE EXPLOSION

Old Fashioned Apple Mini Pies

** Use 2 9" crusts for 12 muffin cups or 24 mini muffin cups.
** Cut the apples into smaller bite-size pieces for mini pies.

Spray muffin pans with Pam. Add a strip of parchment paper to the muffin cup to use as handles for removing the pie easily, if desired. Fill with pie crust as directed below, depending on your mini pie size.

Make the Old Fashioned Apple Pie filling according to this recipe. Only fill muffin cups 3/4 full with pie filling. TOPS - Add lattice pastry strips, use tiny cookie cutters in pastry, top with pie crust (slit top for venting) or just leave the top open. Pinch the crusts together if topping with pie crust.

Mini pies bake a little faster than regular pies. Cook the apple pies for about 15 to 20 minutes at 350 or 375 degrees F. If additional cooking time is needed, check the pies frequently until the crust is golden. Cool in pan.

muffin pan recipe

Muffin/Cupcake Pan: 2-3/4" mini pies

Pie crust: Cut 3-1/2" or 4" circles with a biscuit cutter or use a bowl to cut the circle. Shape the pie crust into each muffin cup.

mini muffin pan recipe

Mini Muffin Pan: 1-3/4" mini pies

Pie Crust: Make the pie crust recipe for Old Fashioned Apple Pie. Roll the dough into 24 balls about 1" in diameter. Press the balls into the bottom and up sides of muffin cups.

Refrigerated Pie Crust: Cut 3" circles with a cookie cutter and shape into each muffin cup.

Apple Mini Pies

Ginger Fruit Pie

Pie Crust:

1 cup fine graham cracker crumbs
3 tablespoons butter or margarine melted

Stir together crumbs and melted butter. Press over bottom and sides of 9 inch pie plate. Chill until set.

Filling:

2 cups tiny marshmallows or 20 large marshmallows
3 tablespoons milk
1 package 3 ounces cream cheese, softened
1 cup sour cream
1 teaspoon vanilla
1/8 teaspoon salt
1 1 lb. can fruit cocktail drained

Melt marshmallows with milk in double boiler, stirring occasionally; cool 10 minutes. Combine cream cheese, sour cream, vanilla and salt. Beat until smooth. Stir in marshmallow mixture and fruit cocktail. Turn into crust. Chill until firm, about 5 hours. Garnish with additional fruit cocktail, if desired.

Magic Blackberry Pie

Pie Crust:

1 cup vanilla wafers, rolled very fine
4 tablespoons melted butter
3/4 cup brown sugar
1/2 teaspoon nutmeg
1/4 teaspoon cinnamon
1/4 teaspoon ginger
1/4 teaspoon all spice

To make crust, combine vanilla wafers rolled very fine, butter, brown sugar, nutmeg, cinnamon, ginger and all spice. Press into an 8" pie pan.

Filling:

1 cup sweetened condensed milk
1/2 cup lemon juice
1 1/2 cups blackberries
1/2 cup heavy cream, whipped
2 tablespoons powdered sugar
1 teaspoon vanilla extract

Prepare 8-inch pie plate with vanilla wafer crumb crust. Combine condensed milk with lemon juice; add blackberries and turn mixture into prepared pie shell. Top with whipped cream that has the powdered sugar and vanilla added.

Swedish Apple Pie

2 1/2 apples sliced and peeled
1/2 teaspoon cinnamon
1 teaspoon sugar
1/4 teaspoon nutmeg
1 cup sugar
3/4 cup melted margarine
1/2 cup chopped pecans
1 cup flour
1 egg
1/8 teaspoon salt

Place sliced apples in container with lid. Sprinkle cinnamon, 1 teaspoon sugar and nutmeg over apples. Close lid and shake until apples are coated. Place apple mixture in greased pie tin or baking dish. In a mixing bowl mix together sugar, margarine, pecans, flour, egg and salt. Pour sugar mixture over apples. Bake at 350 degrees F for 45 minutes to 1 hour until apples are done. Serve with whipped topping or ice cream.

Perfect Cherry Pie

1 unbaked pie shell
4 cups frozen cherries or 2 16 ounces cans pitted tart cherries, drained
1 1/3 cups sugar
1/3 cup flour
1/4 teaspoon almond extract
2 tablespoons butter or margarine

Mix all ingredients together, put in a prepared pie shell. Heat oven to 425 degrees F and bake 35 to 45 minutes. Cover with foil until last 15 minutes.

Perfect Cherry Mini Pies

** Use 2 9" crusts for 12 muffin cups or 24 mini muffin cups.
** Cut the cherries into smaller bite-size pieces for mini pies.

Spray muffin pans with Pam. Add a strip of parchment paper to the muffin cup to use as handles for removing the pie easily, if desired. Fill with pie crust as directed below, depending on your mini pie size.

Make the Cherry Pie filling according to this recipe. Only fill muffin cups 3/4 full with pie filling. TOPS - Add lattice pastry strips, use tiny cookie cutters in pastry, top with pie crust (slit top for venting) or just leave the top open. Pinch the crusts together if topping with pie crust.

Mini pies bake a little faster than regular pies. Cook the cherry pies for about 15 to 20 minutes at 350 or 375 degrees F, then if additional cooking time is needed, check the pies frequently until the crust is golden. Cool in pan.

Muffin/Cupcake Pan: 2-3/4" mini pies

Pie crust: Cut 3-1/2" or 4" circles with a biscuit cutter or use a bowl to cut the circle. Shape the pie crust into each muffin cup.

Mini Muffin Pan: 1-3/4" mini pies

Pie Crust: Make your favorite pie crust recipe. Roll the dough into 24 balls about 1" in diameter. Press the balls into the bottom and up sides of muffin cups.

Refrigerated Pie Crust: Cut 3" circles with a cookie cutter and shape into each muffin cup.

Cranberry Apple Pie

1 unbaked pie shell
4 cups sliced apples
2 cups cranberries
3/4 cup brown sugar
1/4 cup sugar
1/3 cup flour
1 teaspoon cinnamon
2 tablespoons margarine

Mix sugar, brown sugar, flour and cinnamon and mix with the apples and cranberries. Put in 9-inch pie pan on unbaked pie crust. Add margarine scattered on top. Put on top pie crust. Bake 40 to 50 minutes at 425 degrees F.

Cranberry Apple Mini Pies

** Cut the apples into smaller bite-size pieces for mini pies.
** Use 2 9" crusts for 12 muffin cups or 24 mini muffin cups.

Spray muffin pans with Pam. Add a strip of parchment paper to each muffin cup to use as handles for removing the tiny pies easily. Fill with pie crust as directed below, depending on your mini pie size.

Make the Cranberry Apple Pie filling according to this recipe. Only fill muffin cups 3/4 full with pie filling. TOPS - Add lattice pastry strips, use tiny cookie cutters in pastry, top with pie crust (slit top for venting) or just leave the top open. Pinch the crusts together if topping with pie crust.

Mini pies bake a little faster than regular pies. Cook the mini cranberry apple pies for about 15 to 20 minutes at 350 or 375 degrees F. If additional cooking time is needed, check the pies frequently until the crust is golden. Cool in pan.

muffin pan recipe

Muffin/Cupcake Pan: 2-3/4" mini pies

Pie crust: Cut 3-1/2" or 4" circles with a biscuit cutter or use a bowl to cut the circle. Shape the pie crust into each muffin cup.

mini muffin pan recipe

Mini Muffin Pan: 1-3/4" mini pies

Pie Crust: Make your favorite pie crust recipe. Roll the dough into 24 balls about 1" in diameter. Press the balls into the bottom and up sides of muffin cups.

Refrigerated Pie Crust: Cut 3" circles with a cookie cutter and shape into each muffin cup.

Apple Crumb Pie

1 unbaked pie shell
6 large tart apples
1 recipe pastry
1 teaspoon cinnamon
1 cup sugar, divided
3/4 cup flour
1/3 cup margarine

Arrange peeled, sliced apples in pastry lined pan. Mix 1/2 cup of sugar and the cinnamon. Sprinkle over the apples. Sift together the other 1/2 cup of sugar and the flour into a bowl. Cut in the margarine until the mixture is crumbly. Sprinkle over the apples. Bake at 400 degrees F for 40 minutes.

Apple Crumb Mini Pies

** Cut the apples into smaller bite-size pieces for mini pies.
** Use 2 9" crusts for 12 muffin cups or 24 mini muffin cups.

Spray muffin pans with Pam. Add a strip of parchment paper to the muffin cup to use as handles for removing the pie easily, if desired. Refrigerate the crusts in muffin pans for 10 to 15 minutes before filling and baking.

Make the Apple Crumb filling according to this recipe. Only fill muffin cups 3/4 full with filling. Add lattice pastry strips, use tiny cookie cutters in pastry, top with pie crust (slit top for venting) or just leave the top open. Pinch the crusts together if topping with pie crust.

Mini pies bake faster than regular pies. Cook the Apple Crumb pies for about 15 minutes at 400 degrees F, then turn down to 350 degrees F for about 10 to 20 more minutes. Cool in pan.

muffin pan recipe

Muffin/Cupcake Pan: 2-3/4" mini pies

Pie crust: Cut 3-1/2" or 4" circles with a biscuit cutter or use a bowl to cut the circle. Shape the pie crust into each regular size muffin cup.

mini muffin pan recipe

Mini Muffin Pan: 1-3/4" mini pies

Pie Crust: Make your favorite pie crust recipe. Roll the dough into 24 balls about 1" in diameter. Press the balls into the bottom and up sides of mini muffin cups.

Refrigerated Pie Crust: Cut 3" circles using a round cutter and shape into each mini muffin cup or roll the dough into 24 balls about 1" in diameter. Press the balls into the bottom and up sides of mini muffin cups.

Texas Grapefruit Pie

1 baked pie shell
3 large pink grapefruit
2/3 cup granulated sugar
3 teaspoons cornstarch
1 3 ounce package strawberry jello (not sugar free)
1 1/2 cups boiling water
1 9-inch baked pie crust
1 8 ounce carton refrigerated whipped topping or whipped cream

Section grapefruit and peel off membrane. Drain grapefruit well on paper towels, or use a colander to save juice to drink later. Cut sections in half. Mix sugar, corn starch and jello, blending until there are no lumps. Stir mixture into 1 1/2 cups boiling water. Boil mixture until it coats the back of a spoon, 3 to 4 minutes. Let cool. Gently fold grapefruit sections into glaze. Pour into baked pie shell. Refrigerate for 2 hours. Serve topped with refrigerated whipped topping or whipped cream.

Texas Grapefruit Mini Pies

** Use 2 9" crusts for 12 muffin cups or 24 mini muffin cups.
** Refrigerator pie crusts may be used.
** Cut the grapefruit very small for mini pies.
** Add filling from Texas Grapefruit recipe after baking and cooling the mini pie crusts.

Spray muffin pans with Pam. Add a strip of parchment paper to the muffin cup to use as handles for removing the tiny pies easily. Fill muffin cups with pastry as directed below, depending on your mini pie size.

muffin pan recipe

Muffin/Cupcake Pan: 2-3/4" mini pies

Pie crust: Cut 3-1/2" or 4" circles with a biscuit cutter or use a bowl to cut the circle. Shape the pie crust into each regular size muffin cup. Bake at 450 degrees F for 8 to 10 minutes or until lightly browned.

mini muffin pan recipe

Mini Muffin Pan: 1-3/4" mini pies

Pie Crust: Make your favorite pie crust recipe. Roll the dough into 24 balls about 1" in diameter. Press the balls into the bottom and up sides of muffin cups. Bake at 400 degrees F 6 to 8 minutes or until lightly browned.

Refrigerated Pie Crust: Cut 3" circles using a round cutter and shape into each mini muffin cup or roll the dough into 24 balls about 1" in diameter. Press the balls into the bottom and up sides of mini muffin cups. Bake at 400 degrees F 6 to 8 minutes or until lightly browned.

Japanese Fruit Pie

9 inch unbaked pie shell
1 cup sugar
1/2 cup butter
1/8 teaspoon salt
2 eggs, beaten
1 teaspoon vinegar
1/2 cup pecans
1/2 cup raisins
1/2 cup coconut

Cream sugar and butter together. Add salt, eggs and vinegar; beat until well combined. Stir in pecans, raisins and coconut. Pour into unbaked pie shell. Bake at 325 degrees F for 35 to 40 minutes until set.

Japanese Fruit Mini Pies

** Cut the fruit and nuts into smaller bite-size pieces for mini pies.
** Use 2 9" crusts for 12 muffin cups or 24 mini muffin cups.

Spray muffin pans with Pam. Add a strip of parchment paper to each muffin cup to use as handles for removing the tiny pies easily. Fill with pie crust as directed below, depending on your mini pie size.

Make the Japanese Fruit Pie filling according to this recipe. Only fill muffin cups 3/4 full with pie filling. TOPS - Add lattice pastry strips, use tiny cookie cutters in pastry, top with pie crust (slit top for venting) or just leave the top open. Pinch the crusts together if topping with pie crust.

Mini pies bake a little faster than regular pies. Cook the mini fruit pies for about 15 to 20 minutes at 350 or 375 degrees F. If additional cooking time is needed, check the pies frequently until the crust is golden. Cool in pan.

Muffin/Cupcake Pan: 2-3/4" mini pies

Pie crust: Cut 3-1/2" or 4" circles with a biscuit cutter or use a bowl to cut the circle. Shape the pie crust into each muffin cup.

Mini Muffin Pan: 1-3/4" mini pies

Pie Crust: Make your favorite pie crust recipe. Roll the dough into 24 balls about 1" in diameter. Press the balls into the bottom and up sides of muffin cups.

Refrigerated Pie Crust: Cut 3" circles with a cookie cutter and shape into each muffin cup.

Blueberry Peach Pie

Pie Crust:

1 1/4 cup flour
1 teaspoon sugar
1/2 teaspoon salt
1/2 cup silvered almonds
1/2 cup vegetable oil
3 teaspoons water

Mix flour, sugar, salt, almonds, vegetable oil and water together until moistened. Press into pie plate. Bake at 375 degrees F for 20 minutes.

Filling:

3 teaspoons cornstarch
1 cup sugar
1 cup water
1 (3 ounce) package lemon gelatin
3/4 cup frozen or fresh blueberries
4 cups peaches, unpeeled, frozen or fresh, sliced

Combine cornstarch, sugar and water. Bring to a boil and cook for 1 minute, stirring constantly. Remove from heat. Add gelatin and stir until dissolved. Combine blueberries and peaches. Add to gelatin mixture. Toss gently. Pour into cooled baked pie crust. Cover and refrigerate for 1 hour. Serve with whipped cream.

Blueberry Peach Mini Pies

Muffin/Cupcake Pan: 2-3/4" mini pies

Pie crust: Make pastry crust as in recipe above. Form pastry into balls for muffin cups. Spray muffin pan cups with Pam. Add sturdy strips of parchment paper to the muffin cup to use as handles for removing the pie easily. Press pastry into sides and bottom of muffin cups. Bake crust at 350 degrees F for 15 to 20 minutes. Fill with filling recipe.

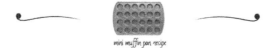

Mini Muffin Pan: 1-3/4" mini pies

Pie crust: Make pastry crust as in recipe above. Form pastry into 24 one inch balls for mini muffin pan. Spray muffin pan cups with Pam. Add a strip of parchment paper to the muffin cup to use as handles for removing the pie easily. Press pastry into sides and bottom of muffin cups. Bake crust at 350 degrees F for 15 to 20 minutes. Fill with filling recipe above.

Backyard Pie

1 unbaked pie shell
2 granny smith apples sliced
1 1/2 cups blackberries
1 1/2 cups raspberries
1 1/2 cups rhubarb
1 1/3 cups unsweetened apple juice
1/2 cup light brown sugar, packed
2 tablespoons honey
1 teaspoon cloves
1 teaspoon grated lemon rind
3 tablespoons cornstarch
1 unbaked 9-inch pie shell

Combine the apples, blackberries, raspberries, rhubarb, apple juice, brown sugar, honey, cloves and lemon rind in a saucepan. Cook until the apples are tender, stirring frequently. Stir in a mixture of the cornstarch and a small amount of water. Cook until thickened. Pour into the pie shell. Bake at 375 degrees F for 35 minutes.

Backyard Mini Pies

** Cut the fruit into smaller bite-size pieces for mini pies.
** Use 2 9" crusts for 12 muffin cups or 24 mini muffin cups.

Spray muffin pans with Pam. Add a strip of parchment paper to each muffin cup to use as handles for removing the tiny pies easily. Fill with pie crust as directed below, depending on your mini pie size.

Make the Backyard Pie filling according to this recipe. Only fill muffin cups 3/4 full with pie filling. TOPS - Add lattice pastry strips, use tiny cookie cutters in pastry, top with pie crust (slit top for venting) or just leave the top open. Pinch the crusts together if topping with pie crust.

Mini pies bake a little faster than regular pies. Cook the mini fruit pies for about 15 to 20 minutes at 350 or 375 degrees F. If additional cooking time is needed, check the pies frequently until the crust is golden. Cool in pan.

muffin pan recipe

Muffin/Cupcake Pan: 2-3/4" mini pies

Pie crust: Cut 3-1/2" or 4" circles with a biscuit cutter or use a bowl to cut the circle. Shape the pie crust into each muffin cup.

mini muffin pan recipe

Mini Muffin Pan: 1-3/4" mini pies

Pie Crust: Make your favorite pie crust recipe. Roll the dough into 24 balls about 1" in diameter. Press the balls into the bottom and up sides of muffin cups.

Refrigerated Pie Crust: Cut 3" circles with a cookie cutter and shape into each muffin cup.

Glaze for Fresh Fruit Pies

1 1/2 cups cold water
1/3 cup sugar
1 teaspoon lemon juice
1 teaspoon cornstarch
Food coloring

Mix sugar and cornstarch. Gradually add water. Cook until thick. Add lemon juice. Pour over fruit. For strawberries use red coloring; for blueberries use blue or purple coloring; for peaches use yellow coloring.

PIES AND MINI PIES: JOIN THE MINI PIE EXPLOSION

Custard Pies

Custard pies are great served warm or cold, plain or garnished with your favorite topping. You'll find mellow, nutmeg-laced egg custard pie, decadent pecan pie and traditional pumpkin pie in this collection of classic custards. There's also a unique recipe for a mock mincemeat pie that will leave your guests asking for your secret to this rich and flavorful filling.

If you're looking for something a bit off the beaten path, try a black raspberry custard or a plum custard pie. Custard pies are popular comfort foods that are easy to prepare and make a welcome addition to any fall dinner or potluck get-together.

Custard Pie Tips

To test a custard pie for doneness, insert a knife an inch or so from the center of the pie. If the blade comes out clean, the filling is cooked through.

Always refrigerate custard pies. The milk and eggs used in the recipe can encourage bacterial growth if left at room temperature for a prolonged period.
Bake custard pies in a water bath to prevent the filling from cracking.

Pies are done when the edges are set and the center still has a little bit of a jiggle. Filling that has puffed up like a soufflé is overcooked.

Double Layer Pumpkin Pie

1 graham cracker crust
1 tablespoon sugar
1 tablespoon milk
4 ounces softened cream cheese
1 1/2 cups refrigerated whipped topping, thawed
1 cup milk
2 4 ounce vanilla instant pudding packages
2 cups canned pumpkin, 16 ounce can
1 teaspoon cinnamon
1/2 teaspoon ground ginger
1/4 teaspoon ground cloves

Mix sugar, milk and cream cheese until smooth. Stir in refrigerated whipped topping. Spread on bottom graham cracker crust. Mix the instant pudding and 1 cup of milk together in a bowl. Beat until well blended, 1 to 2 minutes. Mix in the canned pumpkin and spices. Spread over cream cheese mixture on pie crust. Refrigerate 3 hours.

Coconut Custard Pie

1 unbaked pie shell
4 eggs
1 teaspoon vanilla
1/2 cup sugar
1/4 teaspoon salt
2 1/2 cups milk, scalded
1 cup coconut, divided
1/4 cup brown sugar
2 tablespoons butter

Beat eggs a little and stir in vanilla, sugar, and salt. Then add milk slowly. Add just 1/2 cup of coconut to the egg mixture. Pour into pie shell. Bake in a 400 degrees F oven 30 minutes or until custard is set. Cool. Right before serving, mix brown sugar, 1/2 cup coconut and butter to crumbs and sprinkle on top of pie. Broil until lightly brown.

PIES AND MINI PIES: JOIN THE MINI PIE EXPLOSION

Coconut Custard Mini Pies

** Use 2 9" crusts for 12 muffin cups or 24 mini muffin cups.

Spray muffin pans with Pam. Add a strip of parchment paper to each muffin cup to use as handles for removing the tiny pies easily. Fill with pie crust as directed below, depending on your mini pie size.

Make the Coconut Custard Pie filling according to this recipe. Only fill muffin cups 3/4 full with pie filling. TOPS - Add lattice pastry strips, use tiny cookie cutters in pastry, top with pie crust (slit top for venting) or just leave the top open. Pinch the crusts together if topping with pie crust.

Mini pies bake a little faster than regular pies. Cook the mini coconut pies for about 15 to 20 minutes at 350 or 375 degrees F. If additional cooking time is needed, check the pies frequently until the crust is golden. Cool in pan.

muffin pan recipe

Muffin/Cupcake Pan: 2-3/4" mini pies

Pie crust: Cut 3-1/2" or 4" circles with a biscuit cutter or use a bowl to cut the circle. Shape the pie crust into each muffin cup.

mini muffin pan recipe

Mini Muffin Pan: 1-3/4" mini pies

Pie Crust: Make your favorite pie crust recipe. Roll the dough into 24 balls about 1" in diameter. Press the balls into the bottom and up sides of muffin cups.

Refrigerated Pie Crust: Cut 3" circles with a cookie cutter and shape into each muffin cup.

Old Dutch Shoo-Fly Pie

1 unbaked 9" pie shell
1 1/2 cups flour
1/2 cup light brown sugar
1/4 teaspoon ginger
1 teaspoon cinnamon
1/2 teaspoon cloves
1/4 teaspoon salt
1/4 cup shortening
1 cup boiling water
1 teaspoon baking soda
1 cup molasses or maple syrup

Mix flour, brown sugar, ginger, cinnamon, cloves and salt and blend with shortening. Dissolve baking soda in the hot water and add molasses. Into a 9 inch pie shell, alternately add liquid, crumbs, liquid and crumbs (in just that many additions). Put immediately into pre-heated oven 425 degrees F for 40 minutes.

Plum Custard Pie

1 unbaked 9" pie shell
1 tablespoon flour
1 tablespoon sugar
12 purple plums, cut in half
2 tablespoons sugar
1 tablespoon cinnamon
2 tablespoons butter
1 cup scalded milk
1 tablespoon sugar
1 egg, slightly beaten
1/2 teaspoon vanilla

Line 9 inch pan with rich thin pastry dough. Sprinkle mixture of 1 tablespoon flour and 1 tablespoon sugar on the dough. Place plums in pastry shell. Top with the rest of the ingredients mixed together. Bake in hot oven until crust is brown, 425 degrees F for 15 minutes, then 350 degrees F for 30 minutes until plums are soft.

Pecan Pie

1 unbaked pie shell
1/2 cup sugar
3 tablespoons flour
1/2 teaspoon salt
1 cup pecans, broken
3 eggs – slightly beaten
1/4 cup butter
1 cup white corn syrup

Mix eggs, corn syrup and butter. Then mix sugar, flour and salt and blend in. Add pecans. Pour into unbaked pie shell. Bake for one hour at 350 degrees F.

Pecan Mini Pies

** Chop the pecans into smaller bite-size pieces for mini pies.
** Use 2 9" crusts for 12 muffin cups or 24 mini muffin cups.

Spray muffin pans with Pam. Add a strip of parchment paper to each muffin cup to use as handles for removing the tiny pies easily. Fill with pie crust as directed below, depending on your mini pie size.

Make the Pecan Pie filling according to this recipe. Only fill muffin cups 3/4 full with pie filling. TOPS - Add lattice pastry strips, use tiny cookie cutters in pastry, top with pie crust (slit top for venting) or just leave the top open. Pinch the crusts together if topping with pie crust.

Mini pies bake a little faster than regular pies. Cook the mini pecan pies for about 15 to 20 minutes at 350 or 375 degrees F. If additional cooking time is needed, check the pies frequently until the crust is golden. Cool in pan.

Muffin/Cupcake Pan: 2-3/4" mini pies

Pie crust: Cut 3-1/2" or 4" circles with a biscuit cutter or use a bowl to cut the circle. Shape the pie crust into each muffin cup.

Mini Muffin Pan: 1-3/4" mini pies

Pie Crust: Make your favorite pie crust recipe. (The Mississippi Mud Pie crust recipe in the refrigerated section works well for this mini recipe.) Roll the dough into 24 balls about 1" in diameter. Press the balls into the bottom and up sides of muffin cups.

Refrigerated Pie Crust: Cut 3" circles with a cookie cutter and shape into each muffin cup.

Black Raspberry Custard Pie

1 unbaked 9" pie shell
2 cups milk, scalded
1/2 cup sugar
1 teaspoon vanilla
1/4 teaspoon salt
3 eggs
1 to 2 pints black or red raspberries

Mix the sugar, eggs, vanilla and salt. Temper the egg mixture with a little hot milk and then add the rest of the hot milk. Spread the raspberries over the bottom of a prepared 9 inch pie shell. Then pour the custard over the raspberries. Bake at 400 degrees F for about 5 minutes and then at 325 degrees F for 40 to 50 minutes until set.

PIES AND MINI PIES: JOIN THE MINI PIE EXPLOSION

Black Raspberry Custard Mini Pies

** Cut the raspberries into smaller bite-size pieces for mini pies.
** Use 2 9" crusts for 12 muffin cups or 24 mini muffin cups.

Spray muffin pans with Pam. Add a strip of parchment paper to each muffin cup to use as handles for removing the tiny pies easily. Fill with pie crust as directed below, depending on your mini pie size.

Make the Black Raspberry Custard Pie filling according to this recipe. Only fill muffin cups 3/4 full with pie filling. TOPS - Add lattice pastry strips, use tiny cookie cutters in pastry, top with pie crust (slit top for venting) or just leave the top open. Pinch the crusts together if topping with pie crust.

Mini pies bake a little faster than regular pies. Cook the mini raspberry pies for about 15 to 20 minutes at 350 or 375 degrees F. If additional cooking time is needed, check the pies frequently until the crust is golden. Cool in pan.

muffin pan recipe

Muffin/Cupcake Pan: 2-3/4" mini pies

Pie crust: Cut 3-1/2" or 4" circles with a biscuit cutter or use a bowl to cut the circle. Shape the pie crust into each muffin cup.

mini muffin pan recipe

Mini Muffin Pan: 1-3/4" mini pies

Pie Crust: Make your favorite pie crust recipe. Roll the dough into 24 balls about 1" in diameter. Press the balls into the bottom and up sides of muffin cups.

Refrigerated Pie Crust: Cut 3" circles with a cookie cutter and shape into each muffin cup.

Easy Pumpkin Pie

1 graham cracker crust
1 cup milk
1/2 teaspoon salt
1/2 teaspoon ginger
1/2 teaspoon nutmeg
2/3 cup sugar
1/2 teaspoon cinnamon
1 tablespoon butter
1 egg
1 cup pumpkin

Add all the ingredients and mix well. Pour filling into graham cracker crust.

Easy Pumpkin Mini Pies

mini muffin pan recipe

Graham Cracker Crust for Mini Muffin Pan: 1-3/4" mini pies

2 cups graham cracker crumbs
6 tablespoons butter, melted
5 tablespoons sugar

In a bowl, mix graham cracker crumbs, butter and sugar. Form an oblong ball in your hand by squishing the dough. If the dough doesn't stay together in a ball, more butter might be needed.

Spray muffin pans with Pam. Add a strip of parchment paper to the muffin cup to use as handles for removing the tiny pies easily. Form the dough into balls about 1 1/2" in diameter. Press the balls into the bottom and up sides of muffin cups.

Bake at 325 degrees F for 8 minutes. The crusts need to cool before removing from pan. As they cool, they will form a crust.

Yield: 24 graham cracker mini crusts.

*Note: The Mississippi Mud Pie crust recipe (under refrigerated pies) actually makes a better crust for the pumpkin mini pies. The graham cracker mini crusts will be a little thicker than a regular size pie crust.

Ultimate Caramel Chocolate Pecan Pie

Crust:

2 cups pecans, very finely chopped
1/4 cup sugar
1/4 cup margarine, melted

Filling:

1 14 ounce package caramels (48)
1/4 cup milk
1 cup pecans, chopped
8 squares semi-sweet chocolate (1 package)
1/3 cup milk
1/4 cup powdered sugar
1/2 teaspoon vanilla

Crust: Heat oven to 350 degrees F. Mix pecans, sugar, and margarine. Press onto bottom and sides of 9 inch pie plate. Bake 12 to 15 minutes or until lightly browned. Cool.

Filling: Melt caramels with 1/4 cup milk in heavy saucepan over low heat, stirring frequently, until smooth, or in microwave at 50% power, stirring every 30 seconds. Pour over crust; sprinkle with pecans. Stir chocolate, 1/3 cup milk, powdered sugar, and vanilla in heavy saucepan over very low heat just until melted. Pour over caramel pecan filling, spreading to edges of pie. Refrigerate. Serve with sweetened whipped cream if desired.

Ultimate Caramel Chocolate Pecan Mini Pies

muffin pan recipe

Muffin/Cupcake Pan: 2-3/4" mini pies

Pie crust: Make pastry crust as in recipe above. Form pastry into balls for muffin cups. Spray muffin pan cups with Pam. Add sturdy strips of parchment paper to the muffin cup to use as handles for removing the pie easily. Press pastry into sides and bottom of muffin cups. Bake crust at 325 degrees F for 10 to 15 minutes. Fill with filling recipe.

mini muffin pan recipe

Mini Muffin Pan: 1-3/4" mini pies

Pie crust: Make pastry crust as in recipe above. Be sure pecans are crushed well. Form pastry into 24 one inch balls for mini muffin pan. Spray muffin pan cups with Pam. Add a strip of parchment paper to the muffin cup to use as handles for removing the pie easily. Press pastry into sides and bottom of muffin cups. Bake crust at 325 degrees F for 10 to 15 minutes. Fill with filling recipe above.

Custard Pie

1 unbaked pie shell
4 eggs
1 cup sugar
1 teaspoon vanilla
2 cups warm milk
Nutmeg

Using a wire whisk, beat eggs until foamy. Add sugar and vanilla; beat well. Slowly pour in warm milk, stirring constantly. Pour into pie crust; sprinkle nutmeg on top. Bake at 400 degrees F for 40 to 45 minutes, or until knife inserted halfway from crust to center comes out clean. Serve warm or chilled.

Custard Mini Pies

** Use 2 9" crusts for 12 muffin cups or 24 mini muffin cups.

Spray muffin pans with Pam. Add a strip of parchment paper to each muffin cup to use as handles for removing the tiny pies easily. Fill with pie crust as directed below, depending on your mini pie size.

Make the Custard Pie filling according to this recipe. Only fill muffin cups 3/4 full with pie filling. TOPS - Add lattice pastry strips, use tiny cookie cutters in pastry, top with pie crust (slit top for venting) or just leave the top open. Pinch the crusts together if topping with pie crust.

Mini pies bake a little faster than regular pies. Cook the mini custard pies for about 15 to 20 minutes at 350 or 375 degrees F. If additional cooking time is needed, check the pies frequently until the crust is golden. Cool in pan.

Muffin/Cupcake Pan: 2-3/4" mini pies

Pie crust: Cut 3-1/2" or 4" circles with a biscuit cutter or use a bowl to cut the circle. Shape the pie crust into each muffin cup.

Mini Muffin Pan: 1-3/4" mini pies

Pie Crust: Make your favorite pie crust recipe. Roll the dough into 24 balls about 1" in diameter. Press the balls into the bottom and up sides of muffin cups.

Refrigerated Pie Crust: Cut 3" circles with a cookie cutter and shape into each muffin cup.

Fudge Pecan Pie

1 unbaked pie shell
1/2 cup margarine
3 teaspoons cocoa
3/4 cup hot water
1/8 teaspoon salt
2 cups sugar
1/2 cup flour
1 (5.3 ounces) can evaporated milk
1 teaspoon vanilla
1 cup pecans

Preheat oven and cookie sheet to 350 degrees F. In saucepan, melt margarine, add cocoa and stir until dissolved. Add hot water and stir again. With wire whip, blend in salt, sugar, flour, evaporated milk and vanilla until batter is smooth. Mix in pecans and pour into pie shell. Put on cookie sheet and bake for 50 minutes, or until firm in center. Serve with refrigerated whipped topping.

Batter will be thin and you may think you have done something wrong. There are no eggs and no corn syrup in this recipe, yet the consistency will be very much like pecan pie.

PIES AND MINI PIES: JOIN THE MINI PIE EXPLOSION

Fudge Pecan Mini Pies

** Cut the pecans into smaller bite-size pieces for mini pies.
** Use 2 9" crusts for 12 muffin cups or 24 mini muffin cups.

Spray muffin pans with Pam. Add a strip of parchment paper to each muffin cup to use as handles for removing the tiny pies easily. Fill with pie crust as directed below, depending on your mini pie size.

Make the Fudge Pecan Pie filling according to this recipe. Only fill muffin cups 3/4 full with pie filling. TOPS - Add lattice pastry strips, use tiny cookie cutters in pastry, top with pie crust (slit top for venting) or just leave the top open. Pinch the crusts together if topping with pie crust.

Mini pies bake a little faster than regular pies. Cook the mini fudge pecan pies for about 15 to 20 minutes at 350 or 375 degrees F. If additional cooking time is needed, check the pies frequently until the crust is golden. Cool in pan.

muffin pan recipe

Muffin/Cupcake Pan: 2-3/4" mini pies

Pie crust: Cut 3-1/2" or 4" circles with a biscuit cutter or use a bowl to cut the circle. Shape the pie crust into each muffin cup.

mini muffin pan recipe

Mini Muffin Pan: 1-3/4" mini pies

Pie Crust: Make your favorite pie crust recipe. Roll the dough into 24 balls about 1" in diameter. Press the balls into the bottom and up sides of muffin cups.

Refrigerated Pie Crust: Cut 3" circles with a cookie cutter and shape into each muffin cup.

Graham Cracker Pie

Crust:

1/2 cup butter or margarine
1/2 cup sugar
16 graham crackers, rolled fine

Filling:

1 pint milk
3 egg yolks (reserve whites)
1/2 cup sugar
2 tablespoons cornstarch
1/8 teaspoon salt
2 tablespoons butter
1 teaspoon vanilla

Topping:

3 eggs whites from filling (above)
1/8 teaspoon cream of tartar
4 tablespoons sugar
Cracker crumb mixture (reserved from crust)

For crust, cream together butter and sugar. Mix in graham cracker crumbs. Reserve about 1/2 cup to be sprinkled over pie. Put remainder into pie pan and press firmly. Chill. For filling, cook until thick the milk, egg yolks, sugar, cornstarch, and salt. Add butter and vanilla. Pour into crust. For topping, add cream of tartar to egg whites; beat until stiff. Continue beating, adding the sugar a little at a time. Pile on top of pie. Sprinkle with the reserved crumb mixture from crust. Bake at 400 degrees F until crust hardens and top is browned.

Sour Cream and Blueberry Pie

1 unbaked deep-dish pie shell
2 tablespoons flour
1 cup sour cream
1 teaspoon vanilla extract
1 egg, beaten
3/4 cup sugar
1/4 teaspoon salt
2 1/2 cups fresh blueberries
3 tablespoons flour
3 tablespoons chopped pecans or walnuts
1 1/2 tablespoons butter or margarine

Combine 2 tablespoons flour, sugar, vanilla, egg, sour cream and salt in a mixing bowl; beat at medium speed until smooth. Fold in the blueberries. Spoon into the pie shell. Bake at 400 degrees F for 25 minutes. Combine 3 tablespoons flour, pecans and butter in a bowl and mix well. Sprinkle over the pie. Bake for 10 minutes longer or until brown. Chill until serving time.

Egg Custard Pie

1 unbaked pie shell
1 cup sugar
2 cups milk
6 eggs slightly beaten
1 teaspoon vanilla
Unbaked pie shell

Combine sugar, eggs, milk and vanilla until creamy and smooth. Pour into unbaked pie crust. Bake in 275 degrees F oven until knife comes out clean, approximately 45 minutes. Can be baked in greased baking dish, no crust.

Egg Custard Mini Pies

** Use 2 9" crusts for 12 muffin cups or 24 mini muffin cups.

Spray muffin pans with Pam. Add a strip of parchment paper to each muffin cup to use as handles for removing the tiny pies easily. Fill with pie crust as directed below, depending on your mini pie size.

Make the Egg Custard Pie filling according to this recipe. Only fill muffin cups 3/4 full with pie filling. TOPS - Add lattice pastry strips, use tiny cookie cutters in pastry, top with pie crust (slit top for venting) or just leave the top open. Pinch the crusts together if topping with pie crust.

Mini pies bake a little faster than regular pies. Cook the mini custard pies for about 15 to 20 minutes at 350 or 375 degrees F. If additional cooking time is needed, check the pies frequently until the crust is golden. Cool in pan.

Muffin/Cupcake Pan: 2-3/4" mini pies

Pie crust: Cut 3-1/2" or 4" circles with a biscuit cutter or use a bowl to cut the circle. Shape the pie crust into each muffin cup.

Mini Muffin Pan: 1-3/4" mini pies

Pie Crust: Make your favorite pie crust recipe. Roll the dough into 24 balls about 1" in diameter. Press the balls into the bottom and up sides of muffin cups.

Refrigerated Pie Crust: Cut 3" circles with a cookie cutter and shape into each muffin cup.

Mock Mincemeat Pie

1 unbaked 9 inch double pie crust
4 granny smith apples, peeled, cored, sliced
1 1/2 cups seedless raisins
1/3 cup orange juice
1 tablespoon orange zest
1/2 cup apple cider
1/2 teaspoon ground cloves
3/4 cup sugar
1/2 teaspoon ground cinnamon
2 soda crackers, crushed

Preheat oven to 425 degrees F. Mix the apples, raisins, orange juice, orange zest and apple cider together in a pan. Cook on medium heat, until apples are very soft, stirring occasionally, about 20 minutes. Stir in the cloves, sugar, cinnamon and the soda crackers until well blended. Pour apple mixture into the pie crust. Put on top pie crust, pinch and crimp edges. Prick the top crust in a couple places to vent. Bake in oven for 15 minutes. Reduce oven temperature to 350 degrees F and bake until top is golden brown, about 30 minutes more.

PIES AND MINI PIES: JOIN THE MINI PIE EXPLOSION

Mock Mincemeat Mini Pies

** Cut the fruit into smaller bite-size pieces for mini pies.
** Use 2 9" crusts for 12 muffin cups or 24 mini muffin cups.

Spray muffin pans with Pam. Add a strip of parchment paper to each muffin cup to use as handles for removing the tiny pies easily. Fill with pie crust as directed below, depending on your mini pie size.

Make the Mock Mincemeat Pie filling according to this recipe. Only fill muffin cups 3/4 full with pie filling. TOPS - Add lattice pastry strips, use tiny cookie cutters in pastry, top with pie crust (slit top for venting) or just leave the top open. Pinch the crusts together if topping with pie crust.

Mini pies bake a little faster than regular pies. Cook the mini mock mincemeat pies for about 15 to 20 minutes at 350 or 375 degrees F. If additional cooking time is needed, check the pies frequently until the crust is golden. Cool in pan.

muffin pan recipe

Muffin/Cupcake Pan: 2-3/4" mini pies

Pie crust: Cut 3-1/2" or 4" circles with a biscuit cutter or use a bowl to cut the circle. Shape the pie crust into each muffin cup.

mini muffin pan recipe

Mini Muffin Pan: 1-3/4" mini pies

Pie Crust: Make your favorite pie crust recipe. Roll the dough into 24 balls about 1" in diameter. Press the balls into the bottom and up sides of muffin cups.

Refrigerated Pie Crust: Cut 3" circles with a cookie cutter and shape into each muffin cup.

BONNIE SCOTT

Cream Pies

Cream Pies

You'll find pies for any occasion with this great collection of cream pies. If you're pressed for time, you'll find no bake pies that are a breeze to make with ready-to-serve ingredients and whipped topping for last minute desserts and velvety smooth, feel good cream pies that are perfect for an evening treat after a day of outdoor activities.

From traditional banana or butterscotch cream pie to a magic lemon or topsy-turvy raspberry meringue pie, you'll have rave reviews coming your way when you serve your guests one of these creamy, dreamy pies.

Manse Style Blueberry Cream Pie

1 baked pie shell
1 3 ounce package Philadelphia cream cheese
1 cup heavy cream – whipped
1 teaspoon vanilla
1/2 cup powdered sugar
1 can blueberry pie filling

Soften cream cheese to room temperature. Fold into whipped cream along with vanilla and powdered sugar. Pour into pie shell. Top with blueberry pie filling.

Manse Style Blueberry Mini Pies

** Use 2 9" crusts for 12 muffin cups or 24 mini muffin cups.
** Refrigerator pie crusts may be used.
** Add filling from blueberry recipe after baking and cooling the mini pie crusts.

Spray muffin pans with Pam. Add a strip of parchment paper to the muffin cup to use as handles for removing the tiny pies easily. Fill muffin cups with pastry as directed below, depending on your mini pie size.

Muffin/Cupcake Pan: 2-3/4" mini pies

Pie crust: Cut 3-1/2" or 4" circles with a biscuit cutter or use a bowl to cut the circle. Shape the pie crust into each regular size muffin cup. Bake at 450 degrees F for 8 to 10 minutes or until lightly browned.

Mini Muffin Pan: 1-3/4" mini pies

Pie Crust: Make your favorite pie crust recipe. Roll the dough into 24 balls about 1" in diameter. Press the balls into the bottom and up sides of muffin cups. Bake at 400 degrees F 6 to 8 minutes or until lightly browned.

Refrigerated Pie Crust: Cut 3" circles using a round cutter and shape into each mini muffin cup or roll the dough into 24 balls about 1" in diameter. Press the balls into the bottom and up sides of mini muffin cups. Bake at 400 degrees F 6 to 8 minutes or until lightly browned.

Magic Lemon Cream Pie

1 unbaked graham cracker crumb crust
1 can sweetened condensed milk
1/2 cup lemon juice
2 tablespoons confectioners' sugar
1/4 teaspoon lemon extract or the rind of 1 lemon
1/2 cup whipping cream

Blend together condensed milk, lemon juice and grated lemon rind. Pour into an 8 inch unbaked crumb crust. Fold confectioners' sugar into whipped cream and add to top of pie. Cover with whipped cream – sweetened with confectioners' sugar. Refrigerate.

Raspberry Meringue Pie

3 egg whites
1 cup sugar
1 teaspoon vanilla
14 Ritz crackers, crushed
3/4 cup chopped walnuts
1/2 teaspoon baking powder
1 cup whipping cream
1 package raspberries, frozen, thawed and well drained
3 tablespoons sugar
1 drop of red food coloring

In large bowl, beat egg whites (not real stiff); slowly add 1 cup sugar and beat until stiff; add vanilla. Mix together cracker crumbs, nuts and baking powder. Fold into egg whites mixture. Bake in well greased pie pan for 45 minutes for 325 degrees F. Cool. Whip cream; add sugar, food coloring and raspberries. Pour over pie.

Chocolate Angel Strata Pie

1 unbaked pie shell (9 or 11")

Bake pie shell 12 minutes at 425 degrees F. Cool.

2 egg whites
1/2 teaspoon vinegar
1/4 teaspoon cinnamon
1/4 teaspoon salt
1/2 cup sugar

Beat egg whites, vinegar, cinnamon and salt until soft mounds form. Add sugar slowly, beating until the meringue is in stiff peaks. Spread on sides and bottom of pie shell. Bake at 325 degrees F for 16 to 18 minutes.

Chocolate Whipped Cream Filling:

1 cup chocolate chips
2 egg yolks, slightly beaten
1/4 cup water
1/4 cup sugar
1/4 teaspoon cinnamon
1 cup whipping cream (1 pint)

Melt the chocolate chips in the microwave at 50% power, stirring every 30 seconds. Add the egg yolks and 1/4 cup water. Spread 3 tablespoons of chocolate chip mixture over cooled meringue. Cool remainder of mixture. Combine sugar, cinnamon and whipping cream (1 pint). Beat until thick. Spread half over chocolate in pie shell. Combine remaining whipping cream with chocolate mixture; spread on top. Chill at least 4 hours.

Five Layer Banana Cream Pie

1 cup flour
1/4 cup sugar
1/2 cup margarine
1 cup powdered sugar
Refrigerated whipped topping, 2 small tubs (8 ounces each)
1-8 ounce package cream cheese
4 to 5 bananas
3 cups milk
2 small packages instant pudding mix

Layer #1 (crust): Mix flour, sugar and margarine. Put into a 9x13" pan. Bake for 10 minutes at 350 degrees F; cool. Layer #2: Beat together powdered sugar, cream cheese and 8 ounces refrigerated whipped topping. Put on top of crust.

Layer #3: Slice 4 to 5 bananas on top of 2nd layer. Layer #4: Beat the pudding mixes and milk until thick. Spoon over bananas. Layer #5: Spread 1 small tub of refrigerated whipped topping over 4th layer. Chill 2 hours before serving.

Five Layer Banana Cream Mini Pies

muffin pan recipe

Muffin/Cupcake Pan: 2-3/4" mini pies

Pie crust: Make pastry crust as in recipe above. Form pastry into balls for muffin cups. Spray muffin pan cups with Pam. Add sturdy strips of parchment paper to the muffin cup to use as handles for removing the pie easily. Press pastry into sides and bottom of muffin cups. Bake crust at 325 degrees F for 8 to 10 minutes. Fill with filling recipe.

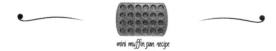

mini muffin pan recipe

Mini Muffin Pan: 1-3/4" mini pies

Pie crust: Make pastry crust as in recipe above. Form pastry into 24 one inch balls for mini muffin pan. Spray muffin pan cups with Pam. Add a strip of parchment paper to the muffin cup to use as handles for removing the pie easily. Press pastry into sides and bottom of muffin cups. Bake crust at 325 degrees F for 8 to 10 minutes. Fill with filling recipe above. Popsicle sticks work well for spreading the filling in the mini cup.

(Note: You can almost half the filling recipe above for mini pie filling.)

Butterscotch Cream Pie

Pie Crust:

1 cup margarine, melted
2 cups flour
2/3 cup pecans, chopped

Pie:

1 cup powdered sugar
1 8 ounce cream cheese
1 12 ounce refrigerated whipped topping
2 small instant butterscotch puddings
3 cups milk
Handful of nuts for top of pie

Make pie crust, put in pan and bake at 350° until lightly browned. Cool. Beat sugar and cream cheese together then fold in 1/2 container of refrigerated whipped topping. Place in pie shell. Beat pudding and milk according to directions. Place on top of cheese layer.

Spread remaining refrigerated whipped topping on top and sprinkle with nuts. Chill. This can also be made using chocolate pudding. Pie can also be used with a graham cracker crust instead.

Butterscotch Cream Mini Pies

Muffin/Cupcake Pan: 2-3/4" mini pies

Pie crust: Make pastry crust as in recipe above. Form pastry into balls for muffin cups. Spray muffin pan cups with Pam. Add sturdy strips of parchment paper to the muffin cup to use as handles for removing the pie easily. Press pastry into sides and bottom of muffin cups. Bake crust at 325 degrees F for 10 minutes or until lightly browned. Fill with filling recipe.

Mini Muffin Pan: 1-3/4" mini pies

Pie crust: Make pastry crust as in recipe above. Form pastry into 24 one inch balls for mini muffin pan. Spray muffin pan cups with Pam. Add a strip of parchment paper to the muffin cup to use as handles for removing the pie easily. Press pastry into sides and bottom of muffin cups. Bake crust at 325 degrees F for 10 minutes or until lightly browned. Fill with filling recipe above. Popsicle sticks work well for spreading the filling in the mini cup.

(Note: You can almost half the filling recipe above for mini pie filling.)

Cherry Cream Pie

1 baked pie shell, 8 or 9"
1 cup powdered sugar
1 3 ounce package cream cheese, softened
1 package Dream Whip®, beaten
1/2 can cherry pie filling

Combine the powdered sugar and cream cheese. Fold in the Dream Whip. Put in baked pie shell. Refrigerate for about an hour; then top with 1/2 can cherry pie filling. Refrigerate again until ready to eat.

Cherry Cream Mini Pies

** Use 2 9" crusts for 12 muffin cups or 24 mini muffin cups.
** Refrigerator pie crusts may be used.
** Add filling from cherry cream recipe after baking and cooling the mini pie crusts.

Spray muffin pans with Pam. Add a strip of parchment paper to the muffin cup to use as handles for removing the tiny pies easily. Fill muffin cups with pastry as directed below, depending on your mini pie size.

muffin pan recipe

Muffin/Cupcake Pan: 2-3/4" mini pies

Pie crust: Cut 3-1/2" or 4" circles with a biscuit cutter or use a bowl to cut the circle. Shape the pie crust into each regular size muffin cup. Bake at 450 degrees F for 8 to 10 minutes or until lightly browned.

mini muffin pan recipe

Mini Muffin Pan: 1-3/4" mini pies

Pie Crust: Make your favorite pie crust recipe. Roll the dough into 24 balls about 1" in diameter. Press the balls into the bottom and up sides of muffin cups. Bake at 400 degrees F 6 to 8 minutes or until lightly browned.

Refrigerated Pie Crust: Cut 3" circles using a round cutter and shape into each mini muffin cup or roll the dough into 24 balls about 1" in diameter. Press the balls into the bottom and up sides of mini muffin cups. Bake at 400 degrees F 6 to 8 minutes or until lightly browned.

Banana Cream Pie

1 baked pie shell
2 eggs beaten
3/4 cup sugar
1/8 teaspoon salt
1/3 cup flour
2 cups hot milk
1 teaspoon vanilla
2 tablespoons butter
3 sliced bananas

Using electric mixer, beat eggs and then add sugar, salt, flour and mix together. Heat milk in a double boiler. Add egg mixture to milk; cook until thick. Remove from heat; add vanilla, butter, bananas. Mix and pour into a baked pie crust. Top with coconut and cool.

Banana Cream Mini Pies

** Use 2 9" crusts for 12 muffin cups or 24 mini muffin cups.
** Refrigerator pie crusts may be used.
** Add filling from banana cream recipe after baking and cooling the mini pie crusts.

Spray muffin pans with Pam. Add a strip of parchment paper to the muffin cup to use as handles for removing the tiny pies easily. Fill muffin cups with pastry as directed below, depending on your mini pie size.

Muffin/Cupcake Pan: 2-3/4" mini pies

Pie crust: Cut 3-1/2" or 4" circles with a biscuit cutter or use a bowl to cut the circle. Shape the pie crust into each regular size muffin cup. Bake at 450 degrees F for 8 to 10 minutes or until lightly browned.

Mini Muffin Pan: 1-3/4" mini pies

Pie Crust: Make your favorite pie crust recipe. Roll the dough into 24 balls about 1" in diameter. Press the balls into the bottom and up sides of muffin cups. Bake at 400 degrees F 6 to 8 minutes or until lightly browned.

Refrigerated Pie Crust: Cut 3" circles using a round cutter and shape into each mini muffin cup or roll the dough into 24 balls about 1" in diameter. Press the balls into the bottom and up sides of mini muffin cups. Bake at 400 degrees F 6 to 8 minutes or until lightly browned.

White Chocolate Coco Cream Pie

2 cups shredded coconut, divided
1/2 cup graham cracker crumbs
1/4 cup butter, softened
2 cups milk
6 egg yolks
3/4 cup sugar
1/2 cup flour
2 tablespoons butter, divided
2 tablespoons crème de cacao
4 ounces white chocolate, melted

Combine 1 cup coconut, the graham cracker crumbs and 1/4 cup butter in a mixing bowl and mix until crumbly. Press over the bottom of a 9-inch pie plate. Bake at 350 degrees F for 10 minutes. Cool on a wire rack. Combine 1 cup coconut and the milk in a saucepan. Bring to a boil over medium heat, stirring frequently. Mix the egg yolks, sugar and flour in a bowl. Mix a small amount of the coconut/milk mix into the egg yolks; stir the eggs into the hot mixture. Bring to a boil and cook for 2 minutes longer, stirring constantly.

Remove from the heat. Stir in 1 tablespoon butter and the crème de cacao. Cool. Spread the white chocolate over the prepared pie shell. Pour the cooled filling over the white chocolate. Chill until just before serving.

Lemon-Blueberry Cream Pie

1 6 ounce shortbread crust prepared
1 4 ounce package sugar-free instant vanilla pudding
1 4 ounce package sugar-free lemon jello
2/3 cup instant powdered milk
1 1/2 cups water
1 cup light whipped topping
1 1/2 cups fresh blueberries

In a bowl, combine pudding, jello, milk powder and water. Mix well using a wire whisk. Blend in 1/4 of whipped topping. Gently fold in blueberries. Spread on crust. Refrigerate for 5 minutes. Spread on the rest of the whipped topping and chill for at least 2 hours.

Frozen Peach Cream Pie

2 6 ounce graham cracker crumb pie crusts
4 fresh peaches, chopped
8 ounces cream cheese
Yellow food coloring
14 ounces sweetened condensed milk
1 teaspoon lemon juice
1/4 teaspoon almond extract
8 ounces frozen, non-dairy whipped topping

In a blender, blend chopped peaches until smooth; set aside. In a mixing bowl, beat the cream cheese until it is fluffy. Beat in sweetened condensed milk, then the mashed peaches, lemon juice, almond extract and food coloring. Mix in whipped topping. Pour in 2 pie crusts. Freeze for 4 hours or until firm. Remove from freezer 5 minutes before serving.

Frozen Peach Cream Mini Pies

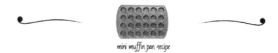

Graham Cracker Crust for Mini Muffin Pan: 1-3/4" mini pies

2 cups graham cracker crumbs
6 tablespoons butter, melted
5 tablespoons sugar

In a bowl, mix graham cracker crumbs, butter and sugar. Form an oblong ball in your hand by squishing the dough. If the dough doesn't stay together in a ball, more butter might be needed.

Spray muffin pans with Pam. Add a strip of parchment paper to the muffin cup to use as handles for removing the tiny pies easily. Form the dough into balls about 1 1/2" in diameter. Press the balls into the bottom and up sides of muffin cups.

Bake at 325 degrees F for 8 minutes. The crusts need to cool before removing from pan. As they cool, they will form a crust.

Yield: 24 graham cracker mini crusts.

Easy Pineapple Cream Pie

1 baked pie shell
24 marshmallows
1 cup crushed pineapple
1 tablespoon lemon juice
1 1/2 cups cream, whipped

In top of double boiler, put marshmallows, crushed pineapple, and lemon juice. Place over boiling water until marshmallows melt. After melting, cool 1/2 hour in refrigerator. Fold in the whipped cream. Pour into shell, and chill.

PIES AND MINI PIES: JOIN THE MINI PIE EXPLOSION

Easy Pineapple Cream Mini Pies

** Use 2 9" crusts for 12 muffin cups or 24 mini muffin cups.
** Refrigerator pie crusts may be used.
** Add filling from pineapple cream recipe after baking and cooling the mini pie crusts.

Spray muffin pans with Pam. Add a strip of parchment paper to the muffin cup to use as handles for removing the tiny pies easily. Fill muffin cups with pastry as directed below, depending on your mini pie size.

muffin pan recipe

Muffin/Cupcake Pan: 2-3/4" mini pies

Pie crust: Cut 3-1/2" or 4" circles with a biscuit cutter or use a bowl to cut the circle. Shape the pie crust into each regular size muffin cup. Bake at 450 degrees F for 8 to 10 minutes or until lightly browned.

mini muffin pan recipe

Mini Muffin Pan: 1-3/4" mini pies

Pie Crust: Make your favorite pie crust recipe. Roll the dough into 24 balls about 1" in diameter. Press the balls into the bottom and up sides of muffin cups. Bake at 400 degrees F 6 to 8 minutes or until lightly browned.

Refrigerated Pie Crust: Cut 3" circles using a round cutter and shape into each mini muffin cup or roll the dough into 24 balls about 1" in diameter. Press the balls into the bottom and up sides of mini muffin cups. Bake at 400 degrees F 6 to 8 minutes or until lightly browned.

Apple Cream Pie

Unbaked pastry for double crust 9 inch pie
2 teaspoons red cinnamon candies
3/4 cup heavy cream
1/2 teaspoon ground cinnamon
2 teaspoons vinegar
1 cup sugar
1/4 cup flour
4 1/2 cups baking apples, thinly sliced, peeled

In a mixing bowl, combine cinnamon candies, cream, cinnamon, vinegar, sugar and flour. Mix well. Add apples and stir gently to mix. Pour into a pastry-lined pie plate. Roll out remaining pastry to fit top of pie. Vent the top crust by cutting vents. Place over apples. Seal the edges. Bake at 400 degrees F for 50 minutes or until apples are tender and pastry is golden.

PIES AND MINI PIES: JOIN THE MINI PIE EXPLOSION

Apple Cream Mini Pies

** Cut the apples into smaller bite-size pieces for mini pies.
** Use 2 9" crusts for 12 muffin cups or 24 mini muffin cups.

Spray muffin pans with Pam. Add a strip of parchment paper to each muffin cup to use as handles for removing the tiny pies easily. Fill with pie crust as directed below, depending on your mini pie size.

Make the Apple Cream Pie filling according to this recipe. Only fill muffin cups 3/4 full with pie filling. TOPS - Add lattice pastry strips, use tiny cookie cutters in pastry, top with pie crust (slit top for venting) or just leave the top open. Pinch the crusts together if topping with pie crust.

Mini pies bake a little faster than regular pies. Cook the mini apple pies for about 15 to 20 minutes at 350 or 375 degrees F. If additional cooking time is needed, check the pies frequently until the crust is golden. Cool in pan.

Muffin/Cupcake Pan: 2-3/4" mini pies

Pie crust: Cut 3-1/2" or 4" circles with a biscuit cutter or use a bowl to cut the circle. Shape the pie crust into each muffin cup.

Mini Muffin Pan: 1-3/4" mini pies

Pie Crust: Make your favorite pie crust recipe. Roll the dough into 24 balls about 1" in diameter. Press the balls into the bottom and up sides of muffin cups.

Refrigerated Pie Crust: Cut 3" circles with a cookie cutter and shape into each muffin cup.

REFRIGERATED PIES

Refrigerated Pies

Whether you use a graham cracker crust, prepared crust or bake a crust from scratch, you'll find tempting fillings to create an easy refrigerator pie that's perfect for impromptu gatherings, potlucks or tasty weekend snacks.

Refrigerated pies are perfect for a busy family. You usually have all the ingredients on hand to whip up a pie in a moment's notice that will satisfy your craving for something sweet. Ingredients from your pantry and refrigerator like canned fruit, flavored gelatin, cream cheese and whipped topping make it simple and easy to serve up a light and refreshing or decadent and rich dessert. Garnish with a sprinkling of chopped nuts, chocolate curls, or a few fresh berries for extra eye-appeal, and your quick and easy dessert is ready to serve.

Please note: A few of the refrigerated pies use raw eggs in their ingredients. Be sure to use fresh eggs if you use raw eggs. We recommend that young children, pregnant women, the elderly and the infirm do not consume raw eggs. Replace the raw eggs with pasteurized eggs or fat-free egg product to eliminate food safety concerns.

French Cherry Pie

9 inch baked pie shell
1 cup sour cream
1 cup milk
1 package 3 1/2 ounce instant vanilla pudding
1/2 teaspoon almond extract
1/2 cup miniature marshmallows
1 can cherry pie filling, 1 pound 5 ounces, chilled

Beat sour cream and milk together – add pudding and extract and mix well. Fold in marshmallows. Pour into pie shell and chill for 45 minutes or more. Spoon cherries on top. Chill. Serve with whipped cream.

French Cherry Mini Pies

** Use 2 9" crusts for 12 muffin cups or 24 mini muffin cups.
** Refrigerator pie crusts may be used.
** Add filling from French Cherry recipe after baking and cooling the mini pie crusts.

Spray muffin pans with Pam. Add a strip of parchment paper to the muffin cup to use as handles for removing the tiny pies easily. Fill muffin cups with pastry as directed below, depending on your mini pie size.

muffin pan recipe

Muffin/Cupcake Pan: 2-3/4" mini pies

Pie crust: Cut 3-1/2" or 4" circles with a biscuit cutter or use a bowl to cut the circle. Shape the pie crust into each regular size muffin cup. Bake at 450 degrees F for 8 to 10 minutes or until lightly browned.

mini muffin pan recipe

Mini Muffin Pan: 1-3/4" mini pies

Pie Crust: Make your favorite pie crust recipe. Roll the dough into 24 balls about 1" in diameter. Press the balls into the bottom and up sides of muffin cups. Bake at 400 degrees F 6 to 8 minutes or until lightly browned.

Refrigerated Pie Crust: Cut 3" circles using a round cutter and shape into each mini muffin cup or roll the dough into 24 balls about 1" in diameter. Press the balls into the bottom and up sides of mini muffin cups. Bake at 400 degrees F 6 to 8 minutes or until lightly browned.

Chocolate Turtle Pie

1 chocolate graham cracker crust
1/3 cup caramel dessert topping
1/3 cup pecans, chopped
2 packs chocolate cook 'n serve pudding (4 ounces each)
3 cups milk

Spread caramel topping over the bottom of the graham cracker crust and sprinkle the caramel with pecans. Put into freezer until firm. Stir the chocolate pudding powder into a pan with milk; cook at medium heat until it comes to a full boil. Remove from heat. Cool for 5 minutes; stir twice. Pour into crust. Cover filling with plastic wrap. Refrigerate overnight.

Cheesecake Pie

Graham cracker crust
1 package cream cheese, 8 ounces, softened
1 tablespoon lemon juice
1/2 cup sugar
1/8 teaspoon salt
1 teaspoon vanilla, divided
2 eggs, beaten
1 cup sour cream
2 tablespoons sugar

Beat the cream cheese until fluffy; slowly blend in lemon juice, 1/2 cup sugar, salt and 1/2 teaspoon vanilla. Add eggs, beating well after each egg. Pour into graham cracker crust and bake in 325 degrees F oven 25 or 30 minutes until set. Combine 1/2 teaspoon vanilla, sour cream and 2 tablespoons sugar and bake 10 minutes longer. Chill several hours.

Chocolate Nut Fluff Pie

Graham cracker crust
6 almond chocolate bars
1/4 cup milk
16 marshmallows
Whipping cream (1/2 pint)

Melt together chocolate bars, milk and marshmallows in double boiler or microwave on 50% power, stirring every 30 seconds. Let mixture cool. Whip whipping cream and add chocolate mixture. Pour into crust and refrigerate until ready to serve.

Chocolate Nut Fluff Mini Pies

mini muffin pan recipe

Graham Cracker Crust for Mini Muffin Pan: 1-3/4" mini pies

2 cups graham cracker crumbs
6 tablespoons butter, melted
5 tablespoons sugar

In a bowl, mix graham cracker crumbs, butter and sugar. Form an oblong ball in your hand by squishing the dough. If the dough doesn't stay together in a ball, more butter might be needed.

Spray muffin pans with Pam. Add a strip of parchment paper to the muffin cup to use as handles for removing the tiny pies easily. Form the dough into balls about 1 1/2" in diameter. Press the balls into the bottom and up sides of muffin cups.

Bake at 325 degrees F for 8 minutes. The crusts need to cool before removing from pan. As they cool, they will form a crust.

Yield: 24 graham cracker mini crusts.

Frozen Lemon Pie

1 cup vanilla wafers, rolled very fine
4 tablespoons melted butter
3/4 cup brown sugar
1/2 teaspoon nutmeg
1/4 teaspoon cinnamon
1/4 teaspoon all spice
1/4 teaspoon ginger
2 egg yolks
3/4 cup sugar
1/3 cup lemon juice
1 tablespoon grated lemon rind
2 egg whites
Canned cream

To make crust, combine vanilla wafers rolled very fine, butter, brown sugar, nutmeg, cinnamon, all spice and ginger.

Filling – Mix egg yolks, sugar, lemon juice and grated lemon rind. Beat egg whites separately and add. Beat 3/4 cup canned cream that has been chilled. Add canned cream last. Put filling in pan that has been lined with crumb mixture. Sprinkle a few crumbs on top for garnish. Freeze fast and serve right from freezer.

Note: Canned cream is not the same as evaporated milk. Both Nestle and Carnation make a product called Table cream or Thick Cream in a can in the baking aisle.

Waikki Pie

Coconut Crust:

3 tablespoons softened butter or margarine
3 cups shredded coconut

Combine butter and coconut. Press evenly into lightly buttered 9" pie plate, building up sides. Bake at 300 degrees F for 20 to 25 minutes or until crust is golden. Cool. Regular pastry shell may be used.

Filling:

1 cup unsweetened pineapple juice
1/2 teaspoon salt
3/4 cup sugar
1 tablespoon lemon juice fresh or frozen
1 envelope unflavored gelatin
1/2 cup cold water
3 well beaten egg yolks
3 stiff beaten egg whites
1/2 cup heavy cream whipped

Combine pineapple juice, salt, sugar and lemon juice. Heat until sugar dissolves. Soften gelatin in cold water. Dissolve in hot mixture. Gradually stir into egg yolks and mix well. Chill until partially set; fold in egg whites and whipped cream. Pour into cooled baked coconut crust. Chill until firm.

French Silk Chocolate Pie

Baked, cooled pie shell or ready-made pie shell

Chocolate Filling:

2 squares unsweetened chocolate (1 ounce each)
1/2 cup butter or margarine
3/4 cup sugar
1 teaspoon vanilla
2 large eggs

Melt the chocolate in microwave at 50% power, stirring every 30 seconds until melted. Let cool. In a small bowl, combine margarine and sugar; blend well. Stir in chocolate and vanilla. Add eggs, beating for 5 minutes after each egg. Pour into cooled pie shell. Chill 2 hours or until firm. Before serving, top with whipped cream and walnuts or pecans, if desired.

French Silk Chocolate Mini Pies

** Use 2 9" crusts for 12 muffin cups or 24 mini muffin cups.
** Refrigerator pie crusts may be used.
** Add filling from French Silk Chocolate recipe after baking and cooling the mini pie crusts.

Spray muffin pans with Pam. Add a strip of parchment paper to the muffin cup to use as handles for removing the tiny pies easily. Fill muffin cups with pastry as directed below, depending on your mini pie size.

muffin pan recipe

Muffin/Cupcake Pan: 2-3/4" mini pies

Pie crust: Cut 3-1/2" or 4" circles with a biscuit cutter or use a bowl to cut the circle. Shape the pie crust into each regular size muffin cup. Bake at 450 degrees F for 8 to 10 minutes or until lightly browned.

mini muffin pan recipe

Mini Muffin Pan: 1-3/4" mini pies

Pie Crust: Make your favorite pie crust recipe. Roll the dough into 24 balls about 1" in diameter. Press the balls into the bottom and up sides of muffin cups. Bake at 400 degrees F 6 to 8 minutes or until lightly browned.

Refrigerated Pie Crust: Cut 3" circles using a round cutter and shape into each mini muffin cup or roll the dough into 24 balls about 1" in diameter. Press the balls into the bottom and up sides of mini muffin cups. Bake at 400 degrees F 6 to 8 minutes or until lightly browned.

Hershey Bar Pie

1 9" graham cracker crust
6 bars 1.45 ounces almond or plain chocolate
18 large marshmallows
1/2 cup milk
2 cups whipped cream

Prepare pie crust. Melt chocolate and marshmallows with milk in double boiler; cool. Fold in whipped cream. Spoon into crust. Refrigerate at least 8 hours. Garnish with additional whipped cream and shaved chocolate if desired.

Hershey Bar Mini Pies

mini muffin pan recipe

Graham Cracker Crust for Mini Muffin Pan: 1-3/4" mini pies

2 cups graham cracker crumbs
6 tablespoons butter, melted
5 tablespoons sugar

In a bowl, mix graham cracker crumbs, butter and sugar. Form an oblong ball in your hand by squishing the dough. If the dough doesn't stay together in a ball, more butter might be needed.

Spray muffin pans with Pam. Add a strip of parchment paper to the muffin cup to use as handles for removing the tiny pies easily. Form the dough into balls about 1 1/2" in diameter. Press the balls into the bottom and up sides of muffin cups.

Bake at 325 degrees F for 8 minutes. The crusts need to cool before removing from pan. As they cool, they will form a crust.

Yield: 24 graham cracker mini crusts.

Mile High Pie

Crust:

1 cup flour
1/2 cup margarine, melted and cooled
1/2 cup chopped pecans
1/4 cup brown sugar

Beat sugar into margarine. Stir in flour and nuts. Spread evenly in a shallow pan. Do not pat down. Bake in preheated over 350 degrees F for 15-20 minutes. Cool. Crumble crust and sprinkle 2/3 of the crumbs in a 13 x 9 dish. Set aside remaining crumbs.

Filling:

2 egg whites
1/4 teaspoon cream of tartar
1/2 cup sugar
10 ounces frozen strawberries, partially thawed
1/2 teaspoon lemon juice
1 1/2 cups refrigerated whipped topping

Beat egg whites with cream of tartar until stiff peaks form. Beat in sugar, strawberries and lemon juice. Beat for 10 minutes. Fold in refrigerated whipped topping. Spread over crumbs, then sprinkle remaining crumbs on top. Cover and freeze. Thaw slightly before serving. Cut into large squares.

Oreo Cookie Pie

3 egg whites
1/8 teaspoon salt
3/4 cup sugar
1 cup crushed Oreo cookies (crumbs)
1/2 teaspoon vanilla
1/2 cup chopped nuts

Beat egg whites with salt. Gradually add sugar and beat until very stiff. Add the cookie crumbs, vanilla and nuts. Put in a buttered 9" pie tin and bake at 325 degrees F for 35 minutes. Top with whipped cream and chocolate shavings or mini chocolate chips.

Daiquiri Pie

1 baked or unbaked graham cracker crust
4 ounce package lemon pudding and pie filling
1/3 cup sugar
3 ounce package lime jello
2 eggs, beaten
2 1/2 cups water
1/2 cup light rum
1 3/4 cups refrigerated whipped topping

Combine pudding powder, sugar and jello in a pan. Mix the eggs with the water. Stir 1/2 cup of the eggs and water into the pudding mixture. Add remaining egg water and bring to a boil over medium heat, stirring constantly. Remove from heat; stir in rum. Blend refrigerated whipped topping into chilled mixture. Spoon into crust and chill 2 hours. Garnish with whipped topping.

Daiquiri Mini Pies

Graham Cracker Crust for Mini Muffin Pan: 1-3/4" mini pies

2 cups graham cracker crumbs
6 tablespoons butter, melted
4 tablespoons sugar

In a bowl, mix graham cracker crumbs, butter and sugar. Form an oblong ball in your hand by squishing the dough. If the dough doesn't stay together in a ball, more butter might be needed.

Spray muffin pans with Pam. Add a strip of parchment paper to the muffin cup to use as handles for removing the tiny pies easily. Form the dough into balls about 1 1/2" in diameter. Press the balls into the bottom and up sides of muffin cups.

Bake at 325 degrees F for 8 minutes. The crusts need to cool before removing from pan. As they cool, they will form a crust.

Yield: 24 graham cracker mini crusts.

Pineapple Jello Pie

Graham cracker crust
1 cup crushed pineapple
12 large marshmallows
3 teaspoons strawberry jello
1 cup whipped cream
2 teaspoons powdered sugar

Heat pineapple and add to marshmallows. Add to jello and cool. Add whipped cream to which 2 teaspoons powdered sugar has been added. Put in graham cracker crust.

Pineapple Jello Mini Pies

mini muffin pan recipe

Graham Cracker Crust for Mini Muffin Pan: 1-3/4" mini pies

2 cups graham cracker crumbs
6 tablespoons butter, melted
4 tablespoons sugar

In a bowl, mix graham cracker crumbs, butter and sugar. Form an oblong ball in your hand by squishing the dough. If the dough doesn't stay together in a ball, more butter might be needed.

Spray muffin pans with Pam. Add a strip of parchment paper to the muffin cup to use as handles for removing the tiny pies easily. Form the dough into balls about 1 1/2" in diameter. Press the balls into the bottom and up sides of muffin cups.

Bake at 325 degrees F for 8 minutes. The crusts need to cool before removing from pan. As they cool, they will form a crust.

Yield: 24 graham cracker mini crusts.

New England Blueberry Pie

9 inch baked pastry shell
4 cups fresh blueberries, divided
1/2 cup granulated sugar
1/2 cup brown sugar, packed
2 1/2 tablespoons flour
2 tablespoons butter or margarine
1 tablespoon lemon juice
1/2 teaspoon allspice
1/2 teaspoon salt
1/4 teaspoon cinnamon
1/8 teaspoon nutmeg
1 cup heavy cream
1/2 teaspoon vanilla

In medium saucepan, combine 2 cups of blueberries with granulated sugar, brown sugar, flour, butter, lemon juice, allspice, salt, cinnamon and nutmeg. Cook and stir over low heat until it comes to a boil. Simmer 5 minutes or until thickened. Stir in remaining 2 cups blueberries. Turn into baked shell and chill. Just before serving, whip cream with vanilla until stiff. Garnish pie and serve.

New England Blueberry Mini Pies

** Use 2 9" crusts for 12 muffin cups or 24 mini muffin cups.
** Refrigerator pie crusts may be used.
** Add filling from blueberry recipe after baking and cooling the mini pie crusts.

Spray muffin pans with Pam. Add a strip of parchment paper to the muffin cup to use as handles for removing the tiny pies easily. Fill muffin cups with pastry as directed below, depending on your mini pie size.

muffin pan recipe

Muffin/Cupcake Pan: 2-3/4" mini pies

Pie crust: Cut 3-1/2" or 4" circles with a biscuit cutter or use a bowl to cut the circle. Shape the pie crust into each regular size muffin cup. Bake at 450 degrees F for 8 to 10 minutes or until lightly browned.

mini muffin pan recipe

Mini Muffin Pan: 1-3/4" mini pies

Pie Crust: Make your favorite pie crust recipe. Roll the dough into 24 balls about 1" in diameter. Press the balls into the bottom and up sides of muffin cups. Bake at 400 degrees F 6 to 8 minutes or until lightly browned.

Refrigerated Pie Crust: Cut 3" circles using a round cutter and shape into each mini muffin cup or roll the dough into 24 balls about 1" in diameter. Press the balls into the bottom and up sides of mini muffin cups. Bake at 400 degrees F 6 to 8 minutes or until lightly browned.

Heavenly Yogurt Pie

1 graham cracker pie shell
8 ounces lemon yogurt
8 ounces orange-pineapple yogurt
8 ounces refrigerated whipped topping
Crushed pineapple, 20 ounce can, well drained

Mix yogurts, refrigerated whipped topping and pineapple. Place in graham cracker pie shell. Shave semi-sweet chocolate curls on top for decoration, if desired. Chill for 3 hours.

Heavenly Yogurt Mini Pies

mini muffin pan recipe

Graham Cracker Crust for Mini Muffin Pan: 1-3/4" mini pies

2 cups graham cracker crumbs
6 tablespoons butter, melted
4 tablespoons sugar

In a bowl, mix graham cracker crumbs, butter and sugar. Form an oblong ball in your hand by squishing the dough. If the dough doesn't stay together in a ball, more butter might be needed.

Spray muffin pans with Pam. Add a strip of parchment paper to the muffin cup to use as handles for removing the tiny pies easily. Form the dough into balls about 1 1/2" in diameter. Press the balls into the bottom and up sides of muffin cups.

Bake at 325 degrees F for 8 minutes. The crusts need to cool before removing from pan. As they cool, they will form a crust.

Yield: 24 graham cracker mini crusts.

Marvelous Mocha Pie

20 Oreo cookies, crushed
1/4 cup melted butter
1 quart coffee ice cream
3 squares chocolate, unsweetened
1/4 cup butter
2/3 cup sugar
1 small can evaporated milk

Crush cookies, add melted butter. Mix and put in 9-inch pie tin to make a crust. Spread softened ice cream in crust. Freeze. Combine chocolate, butter and sugar. When this has melted, add evaporated milk and cook until thick. Cool and spread over ice cream. Return to freezer. Serve with dollop of whipped cream.

Key Lime Pie

Graham cracker pie shell (9 inch)
Knox gelatin (1 envelope)
1/4 teaspoon salt
1/2 cup sugar
1/2 cup lime juice
4 tablespoons of water
4 egg yolks
1 teaspoon lime peel (grated)
Few drops of food coloring (green)
4 egg whites
1/2 cup sugar
1 cup cream, whipped

In a pan, place gelatin, salt and sugar and mix well. Beat the lime juice, water and 4 egg yolks and stir into gelatin mixture. While constantly stirring, cook the mixture over medium heat until boiling, then remove from heat. Mix in the grated peel. Add the green food coloring (sparingly).

Chill mixture, stirring occasionally until the mixture slightly mounds. Beat the 4 egg whites and slowly pour in sugar to form stiff peaks. Fold the gelatin mixture into the beaten egg whites, then fold in the whipped cream. Evenly spread the mixture into pie shell and chill. Once chilled, top with whipped cream and grated lime if desired.

Cherry Cheese Pie

1 graham cracker pie crust
8 ounces cream cheese
8 ounces powdered sugar
8 ounces refrigerated whipped topping
21 ounce can cherry pie filling

Cream the cream cheese and powdered sugar together. Fold in the refrigerated whipped topping. Pour into a ready-made graham cracker crust. Top with canned cherry pie filling, or substitute any other flavor of pie filling. Place in refrigerator to set, for at least 1 hour.

Cherry Cheese Mini Pies

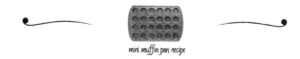

mini muffin pan recipe

Graham Cracker Crust for Mini Muffin Pan: 1-3/4" mini pies

2 cups graham cracker crumbs
6 tablespoons butter, melted
4 tablespoons sugar

In a bowl, mix graham cracker crumbs, butter and sugar. Form an oblong ball in your hand by squishing the dough. If the dough doesn't stay together in a ball, more butter might be needed.

Spray muffin pans with Pam. Add a strip of parchment paper to the muffin cup to use as handles for removing the tiny pies easily. Form the dough into balls about 1 1/2" in diameter. Press the balls into the bottom and up sides of muffin cups.

Bake at 325 degrees F for 8 minutes. The crusts need to cool before removing from pan. As they cool, they will form a crust.

Yield: 24 graham cracker mini crusts.

Lemonade Pie

2 9 inch graham cracker crusts
6 ounce can of frozen lemonade
8 ounces refrigerated whipped topping
1 can sweetened condensed milk
1 lemon

Mix the lemonade, refrigerated whipped topping and condensed milk in a bowl until smooth. Divide and place into 2 pie shells and freeze. Slice and serve garnished with a lemon slice.

Lemonade Mini Pies

mini muffin pan recipe

Graham Cracker Crust for Mini Muffin Pan: 1-3/4" mini pies

2 cups graham cracker crumbs
6 tablespoons butter, melted
4 tablespoons sugar

In a bowl, mix graham cracker crumbs, butter and sugar. Form an oblong ball in your hand by squishing the dough. If the dough doesn't stay together in a ball, more butter might be needed.

Spray muffin pans with Pam. Add a strip of parchment paper to the muffin cup to use as handles for removing the tiny pies easily. Form the dough into balls about 1 1/2" in diameter. Press the balls into the bottom and up sides of muffin cups.

Bake at 325 degrees F for 8 minutes. The crusts need to cool before removing from pan. As they cool, they will form a crust.

Yield: 24 graham cracker mini crusts.

German Chocolate Pie

Crust:

2 egg whites
1/8 teaspoon salt
1/8 teaspoon cream of tartar
1/2 cup sugar
1/2 cup chopped pecans or walnuts, optional
1/2 teaspoon vanilla

Filling:

4 ounce package German sweet chocolate
3 teaspoons water
2 egg yolks
1 teaspoon vanilla
1 teaspoon powdered sugar
1 cup whipping cream

Beat egg whites, salt and cream of tartar until it forms soft peaks. Add sugar gradually and continue beating until mixture is very stiff. Fold in 1/2 teaspoon vanilla and nuts. Turn into lightly greased 8" pie pan and make a nest-like shell. Bake at 300 degrees F for 50-55 minutes. Cool.

For filling: Place chocolate & water in saucepan over low heat. Stir until melted. Add egg yolks, sugar & vanilla. Cool. Whip cream and stir into chocolate mixture. Spoon into meringue. Top with additional whipped cream and chocolate & white chocolate shavings. Chill 3 hours before serving.

German Chocolate Mini Pies

Muffin/Cupcake Pan: 2-3/4" mini pies

Pie crust: Make pastry crust as in recipe above. Form pastry into balls for muffin cups. Spray muffin pan cups with Pam. Add sturdy strips of parchment paper to the muffin cup to use as handles for removing the pie easily. Press pastry into sides and bottom of muffin cups. Bake crust at 300 degrees F for 40 minutes or longer. Fill with filling recipe above.

Mini Muffin Pan: 1-3/4" mini pies

Pie crust: Make pastry crust as in recipe above. Form pastry into 24 one inch balls for mini muffin pan. Spray muffin pan cups with Pam. Add a strip of parchment paper to the muffin cup to use as handles for removing the pie easily. Press pastry into sides and bottom of muffin cups. Bake crust at 300 degrees F for 30 minutes or longer.

Cool crust. Fill with filling recipe above. A popsicle stick works great for spreading the filling in the mini muffin cups.

Mexican Fiesta Pie

6 teaspoons butter, melted
3 teaspoons sugar
1 1/2 cups pretzels, finely ground
1 quart vanilla ice milk, softened
1/2 10 ounce can frozen margarita concentrate, thawed
Lime twists, optional

Heat oven to 350 degrees F. Combine butter, sugar and pretzels; pat into 9 inch glass pie plate, reserving 2 T. for topping. Bake 10 minutes. Cool. Blend ice milk and 5 oz. of margarita concentrate until thoroughly combined. Spoon into crust. Sprinkle with remaining crumbs. Freeze. Garnish with lime twists.

Mexican Fiesta Mini Pies

muffin pan recipe

Muffin/Cupcake Pan: 2-3/4" mini pies

Pie crust: Make pastry crust as in recipe above. Form pastry into balls for muffin cups. Spray muffin pan cups with Pam. Add sturdy strips of parchment paper to the muffin cup to use as handles for removing the pie easily. Press pastry into sides and bottom of muffin cups. Bake crust at 350 degrees F for 8 minutes. Fill with filling recipe above.

mini muffin pan recipe

Mini Muffin Pan: 1-3/4" mini pies

Pie crust: Make pastry crust as in recipe above. Form pastry into 24 one inch balls for mini muffin pan. Spray muffin pan cups with Pam. Add a strip of parchment paper to the muffin cup to use as handles for removing the pie easily. Press pastry into sides and bottom of muffin cups. Bake crust at 325 degrees F for 8 minutes.

Cool crust. Fill with filling recipe above. A popsicle stick works great for spreading the filling in the mini muffin cups.

Grasshopper Pie

Pie crust:

16 graham crackers or chocolate wafers, crushed
3 tablespoons butter
1/3 cup sugar

Mix and spread evenly in a pie pan.

Filling:

1/2 cup milk
25 regular size marshmallows
1/2 pint cream
1 oz. green crème de menthe
1/2 oz. cream de cocoa

Heat milk, add marshmallows and stir until melted. Set aside to cool. Whip cream and add crème de menthe and crème de cocoa. Whip again. Fold into first mixture. Pour into pie shell and refrigerate 6 hours or overnight. Serve with dab of whipped cream topped with a cherry or strawberry.

French Chocolate Pie

Pie crust:

Spread butter **very thickly** in pie plate. Press shredded coconut in the butter until the pie plate is coated with a thick layer. Bake at 250 or 300 degrees F until golden. Cool.

Filling:

1 cup sugar
1 cup butter
2 tablespoons instant coffee
1 cup nuts, coarsely chopped
2 eggs
Unsweetened chocolate, 3 ounces, melted
Brandy or rum to taste (optional)

Cream sugar and butter. Add eggs one at a time, beating 2 minutes between each egg addition. Add coffee, nuts, cooled chocolate and rum or brandy. Pour into pie shell and chill.

Pumpkin Chiffon Pie

1 baked pie shell
1 cup pumpkin, canned
3/8 cup granulated sugar
1/4 cup brown sugar
1/2 teaspoon salt
1 teaspoon cinnamon
1/4 teaspoon nutmeg
2/3 cup fresh milk
2 teaspoons butter
2 1/2 tablespoons cornstarch
3 tablespoons milk
3 egg whites
1 3/4 tablespoons sugar

Mix pumpkin with 3/8 cup of granulated sugar, brown sugar, salt, cinnamon, nutmeg, milk and butter; bring to a boil. Add cornstarch dissolved in 3 tablespoons of milk. Cook until the mixture thickens. Remove from stove. Place egg whites in a mixing bowl, add 1 3/4 tablespoons of sugar to the beaten egg whites and continue beating one minute.

Slowly pour cooked pumpkin mix over beaten egg whites and fold gently together with a hand wire beater, mixing well. Place hot filling in baked pie shell. Fill the shell generously and place in ice box to chill. Top with whipped cream before serving.

Pumpkin Chiffon Mini Pies

** Use 2 9" crusts for 12 muffin cups or 24 mini muffin cups.
** Refrigerator pie crusts may be used.
** Add filling from pumpkin chiffon recipe after baking and cooling the mini pie crusts.

Spray muffin pans with Pam. Add a strip of parchment paper to the muffin cup to use as handles for removing the tiny pies easily. Fill muffin cups with pastry as directed below, depending on your mini pie size.

muffin pan recipe

Muffin/Cupcake Pan: 2-3/4" mini pies

Pie crust: Cut 3-1/2" or 4" circles with a biscuit cutter or use a bowl to cut the circle. Shape the pie crust into each regular size muffin cup. Bake at 450 degrees F for 8 to 10 minutes or until lightly browned.

mini muffin pan recipe

Mini Muffin Pan: 1-3/4" mini pies

Pie Crust: Make your favorite pie crust recipe. (The pastry recipe for the Mississippi Mud Pie in the Refrigerated Pies section makes a perfect crust for this recipe.) Roll the dough into 24 balls about 1" in diameter. Press the balls into the bottom and up sides of muffin cups. Bake at 400 degrees F 6 to 8 minutes or until lightly browned.

Pumpkin Ice Cream Pie

Baked pie shell
1 quart vanilla ice cream
1/2 cup brown sugar
1 cup pumpkin
1 teaspoon cinnamon
1 teaspoon ginger

Soften ice cream, add remaining ingredients. Pour into crust. Store in freezer several hours before serving.

Pumpkin Ice Cream Mini Pies

** Use 2 9" crusts for 12 muffin cups or 24 mini muffin cups.
** Refrigerator pie crusts may be used.
** Add filling from pumpkin recipe after baking and cooling the mini pie crusts.

Spray muffin pans with Pam. Add a strip of parchment paper to the muffin cup to use as handles for removing the tiny pies easily. Fill muffin cups with pastry as directed below, depending on your mini pie size.

muffin pan recipe

Muffin/Cupcake Pan: 2-3/4" mini pies

Pie crust: Cut 3-1/2" or 4" circles with a biscuit cutter or use a bowl to cut the circle. Shape the pie crust into each regular size muffin cup. Bake at 450 degrees F for 8 to 10 minutes or until lightly browned.

mini muffin pan recipe

Mini Muffin Pan: 1-3/4" mini pies

Pie Crust: Make your favorite pie crust recipe. (The pastry recipe for the Mississippi Mud Pie in the Refrigerated Pies section makes a perfect crust for this recipe.) Roll the dough into 24 balls about 1" in diameter. Press the balls into the bottom and up sides of muffin cups. Bake at 400 degrees F 6 to 8 minutes or until lightly browned.

Refrigerated Pie Crust: Cut 3" circles using a round cutter and shape into each mini muffin cup or roll the dough into 24 balls about 1" in diameter. Press the balls into the bottom and up sides of mini muffin cups. Bake at 400 degrees F 6 to 8 minutes or until lightly browned.

Mississippi Mud Pie

Crust:

1 cup flour
1/2 cup butter
1/2 cup ground pecans

Cream together all crust ingredients (save some nuts to sprinkle on top). Pat into a 9x13 inch pan with fingers. Bake at 350 degrees F for 20 minutes. Cool.

Filling:

Cream cheese (8 oz.), softened
13 oz. refrigerated whipped topping
1 cup powdered sugar
3 cups milk
1 large box instant chocolate pudding

Cream together powdered sugar, cream cheese and 1 cup refrigerated whipped topping. Spread the mixture on top of cooled crust. Beat pudding into milk with whisk for 2 minutes and lay on top of cream cheese mixture. Put the rest of the refrigerated whipped topping on top of pudding. Sprinkle with remaining nuts or chocolate sprinkles and refrigerate.

Mississippi Mud Mini Pies

Muffin/Cupcake Pan: 2-3/4" mini pies

Pie crust: Make pastry crust as in recipe above. Form pastry into balls for muffin cups. Spray muffin pan cups with Pam. Add sturdy strips of parchment paper to the muffin cup to use as handles for removing the pie easily. Press pastry into sides and bottom of muffin cups. Bake crust at 350 degrees F for 20 minutes. This recipe works perfectly if the muffin cups are sprayed with Pam and the parchment paper handles are added. Fill with filling recipe above.

Mini Muffin Pan: 1-3/4" mini pies

Pie crust: Make pastry crust as in recipe above. Form pastry into 24 one inch balls for mini muffin pan. Spray muffin pan cups with Pam. Add a strip of parchment paper to the muffin cup to use as handles for removing the pie easily. Press pastry into sides and bottom of muffin cups. Bake crust at 325 degrees F for 20 minutes. Crust will be fragile but this recipe works perfectly if the muffin cups are sprayed with Pam and the 5" parchment paper handles are added.

Cool crust. Fill with filling recipe above. A popsicle stick works great for spreading the filling in the mini muffin cups.

Mississippi Mud Mini Pies

Peppermint Fudge Pie

24 crushed cream filled chocolate cookies (2 cups)
1/3 cup melted margarine

Press above into 9" pie tin. Chill.

4 1/2 cups miniature marshmallows
1/2 cup milk
Red food coloring
1 cup heavy whipping cream (whip until peaks)
1/2 cup finely crushed peppermint candy

Melt 3 cups mini marshmallows and milk; stir until smooth. Refrigerate until thickened slightly. Mix until well blended. Tint with few drops food coloring, fold in whipped cream, candy and remaining marshmallows. Put into crust. Wrap in plastic wrap. Freeze. Unwrap and place in refrigerator 1/2 hour before serving.

Frozen Raspberry Pie

1 baked pie shell
10 ounce package frozen raspberries, thawed
2 egg whites, room temperature
1 teaspoon lemon juice
1 cup sugar
1/8 teaspoon salt
1 cup cream, whipped
1/4 cup roasted almonds, chopped

Mix raspberries (reserve a few raspberries for decoration), egg whites, lemon juice, sugar and salt. Beat for 15 minutes or until mixture is stiff. Fold in almonds and whipped cream. Mound in baked pie shell. Freeze until firm. Garnish with reserved raspberries.

Frozen Raspberry Mini Pies

** Use 2 9" crusts for 12 muffin cups or 24 mini muffin cups.
** Refrigerator pie crusts may be used.
** Add filling from raspberry recipe after baking and cooling the mini pie crusts.

Spray muffin pans with Pam. Add a strip of parchment paper to the muffin cup to use as handles for removing the tiny pies easily. Fill muffin cups with pastry as directed below, depending on your mini pie size.

muffin pan recipe

Muffin/Cupcake Pan: 2-3/4" mini pies

Pie crust: Cut 3-1/2" or 4" circles with a biscuit cutter or use a bowl to cut the circle. Shape the pie crust into each regular size muffin cup. Bake at 450 degrees F for 8 to 10 minutes or until lightly browned.

mini muffin pan recipe

Mini Muffin Pan: 1-3/4" mini pies

Pie Crust: Make your favorite pie crust recipe. Roll the dough into 24 balls about 1" in diameter. Press the balls into the bottom and up sides of muffin cups. Bake at 400 degrees F 6 to 8 minutes or until lightly browned.

Refrigerated Pie Crust: Cut 3" circles using a round cutter and shape into each mini muffin cup or roll the dough into 24 balls about 1" in diameter. Press the balls into the bottom and up sides of mini muffin cups. Bake at 400 degrees F 6 to 8 minutes or until lightly browned.

Bavarian Mint Pie

1 vanilla wafer or graham cracker crust
1/2 cup butter
3/4 cup sugar
3 eggs
2 squares unsweetened chocolate
1 bar German's sweet chocolate
1 teaspoon mint flavoring

Melt the 2 chocolates together in double boiler. Cream butter and sugar until smooth as whipped cream. Beat eggs until extremely light and frothy. Add to butter and sugar. Add melted chocolate and stir until very smooth. Add mint flavoring, stir well. Turn into cooled crumb crust. When firm, top with:

1 cup whipping cream
2 tablespoons powdered sugar
1/4 teaspoon mint flavoring

Whip together. Refrigerate.

Norwegian Pie

1 cup flour
1 1/2 cups sugar
1/4 teaspoon salt
2 teaspoons baking powder
2 eggs, beaten
1/2 teaspoon vanilla
2 cups chopped apples
1 cup chopped nuts

Combine flour, sugar, salt and baking powder. Add eggs, vanilla, apples and nuts. Mix well. This will be a stiff batter. Spread evenly in 2 greased 8 inch pie plates. Bake for 30 to 40 minutes in 350 degrees F oven. Serve with whipped topping or ice cream.

Peanut Butter Pie

2 graham cracker pie crusts
8 ounce package cream cheese, softened
1 cup powdered sugar
1/4 cup crunchy peanut butter
1/2 cup milk
1/4 cup peanut halves
8 ounce container whipped topping

Whip cream cheese until soft and fluffy. Beat in peanut butter and sugar. Gradually add milk. Fold in whipped topping. Put into the pie crusts. Sprinkle tops with peanuts. Freeze.

Peanut Butter Mini Pies

Graham Cracker Crust for Mini Muffin Pan: 1-3/4" mini pies

2 cups graham cracker crumbs
6 tablespoons butter, melted
4 tablespoons sugar

In a bowl, mix graham cracker crumbs, butter and sugar. Form an oblong ball in your hand by squishing the dough. If the dough doesn't stay together in a ball, more butter might be needed.

Spray muffin pans with Pam. Add a strip of parchment paper to the muffin cup to use as handles for removing the tiny pies easily. Form the dough into balls about 1 1/2" in diameter. Press the balls into the bottom and up sides of muffin cups.

Bake at 325 degrees F for 8 minutes. The crusts need to cool before removing from pan. As they cool, they will form a crust.

Yield: 24 graham cracker mini crusts.

Miscellaneous Pies

Coffee Bavarian Pie

1 9 inch graham cracker or chocolate wafer crust
1 envelope unflavored gelatin
1 tablespoon instant coffee
1/2 cup cold water
1/2 cup sugar
1/4 teaspoon salt
1 12 oz. can evaporated milk

Soften gelatin in the cold water in a 1-quart saucepan. Add the sugar, instant coffee and salt. Stir over medium heat until gelatin and sugar dissolve. Remove from heat. Stir in 1 cup of the evaporated milk. Chill in a large mixing bowl until firm (2-3 hours). At low speed, beat until mixture is broken up. Add remaining evaporated milk and beat at high speed until mixture fills bowl. Pour into crust and chill until firm.

Sweet Potato Chiffon Pie

1 graham cracker pie shell
2 egg whites
2 egg yolks
2 cups mashed sweet potatoes
Juice of 1/2 orange
1/2 teaspoon salt
1/2 cup milk
1/2 cup corn syrup
2 tablespoons margarine, melted
1 teaspoon grated orange rind

Beat egg whites until stiff. Combine all other ingredients. Fold in egg whites. Pour into pie shell. Bake at 350 degrees F for 35 minutes.

Sweet Potato Mini Pies

mini muffin pan recipe

Graham Cracker Crust for Mini Muffin Pan: 1-3/4" mini pies

2 cups graham cracker crumbs
6 tablespoons butter, melted
4 tablespoons sugar

In a bowl, mix graham cracker crumbs, butter and sugar. Form an oblong ball in your hand by squishing the dough. If the dough doesn't stay together in a ball, more butter might be needed.

Spray muffin pans with Pam. Add a strip of parchment paper to the muffin cup to use as handles for removing the tiny pies easily. Form the dough into balls about 1 1/2" in diameter. Press the balls into the bottom and up sides of muffin cups.

Bake at 325 degrees F for 8 minutes. The crusts need to cool before removing from pan. As they cool, they will form a crust.

Yield: 24 graham cracker mini crusts.

Country Molasses Pie

1 unbaked pie shell
3/4 cup flour
1/2 cup sugar
1 tablespoon butter
1/4 teaspoon baking soda
1/4 cup boiling water
1/4 cup molasses

Combine flour and sugar. Cut in butter until very fine. Set aside. Combine baking soda, water and molasses. Beat until it becomes foamy and rises. Add the crumb mixture. Mix well. Pour into pastry-lined pie pan. Bake at 350 degrees F for 35 minutes or until set firm.

This recipe has a cake-like texture.

PIES AND MINI PIES: JOIN THE MINI PIE EXPLOSION

Country Molasses Mini Pies

** Use 2 9" crusts for 12 muffin cups or 24 mini muffin cups.

Spray muffin pans with Pam. Add a strip of parchment paper to each muffin cup to use as handles for removing the tiny pies easily. Fill with pie crust as directed below, depending on your mini pie size.

Make the Country Molasses Pie filling according to this recipe. Only fill muffin cups 3/4 full with pie filling. TOPS - Add lattice pastry strips, use tiny cookie cutters in pastry, top with pie crust (slit top for venting) or just leave the top open. Pinch the crusts together if topping with pie crust.

Mini pies bake a little faster than regular pies. Cook the mini molasses pies for about 15 to 20 minutes at 350 or 375 degrees F. If additional cooking time is needed, check the pies frequently until the crust is golden. Cool in pan.

Muffin/Cupcake Pan: 2-3/4" mini pies

Pie crust: Cut 3-1/2" or 4" circles with a biscuit cutter or use a bowl to cut the circle. Shape the pie crust into each muffin cup.

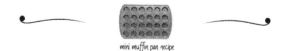

Mini Muffin Pan: 1-3/4" mini pies

Pie Crust: Make your favorite pie crust recipe. Roll the dough into 24 balls about 1" in diameter. Press the balls into the bottom and up sides of muffin cups.

Refrigerated Pie Crust: Cut 3" circles with a cookie cutter and shape into each muffin cup.

Chocolate Peanut Butter Ice Cream Pie

1 1/2 cups graham cracker crumbs
1/4 cup butter, melted
3 tablespoons sugar
2 tablespoons salted peanuts, chopped

Filling:

2 cups chocolate ice cream, slightly softened
4 cups vanilla ice cream, slightly softened
1/3 cup peanut butter
2 tablespoons salted peanuts
Chocolate syrup

Preheat oven to 350 degrees F. In a small bowl, stir together graham cracker crumbs, butter, sugar and 2 tablespoons chopped peanuts to make crust. Press into a 9 or 10 inch pie pan and up the sides. Bake for 6 to 8 minutes. Cool completely. Spread chocolate ice cream into cooled pie shell. Freeze for 30 minutes.

Meanwhile, in a large bowl, mix vanilla ice cream and peanut butter; mix well. Freeze mixture for 30 minutes. Spoon peanut butter mixture over frozen chocolate layer. Spread to edges, mounding it slightly in the middle. Sprinkle with 2 tablespoons of peanuts. Freeze for 4 to 5 hours. Let stand for 5 minutes at room temperature before serving. Drizzle with chocolate syrup to garnish before serving.

Chocolate Peanut Butter Mini Pies

muffin pan recipe

Muffin/Cupcake Pan: 2-3/4" mini pies

Pie crust: Make pastry crust as in recipe above. Form pastry into balls for muffin cups. Spray muffin pan cups with Pam. Add sturdy strips of parchment paper to the muffin cup to use as handles for removing the pie easily. Press pastry into sides and bottom of muffin cups. Bake crust at 325 degrees F for 6 to 8 minutes. Fill with filling recipe above.

mini muffin pan recipe

Mini Muffin Pan: 1-3/4" mini pies

Pie crust: Make pastry crust as in recipe above. Form pastry into 24 one inch balls for mini muffin pan. Spray muffin pan cups with Pam. Add a strip of parchment paper to the muffin cup to use as handles for removing the pie easily. Press pastry into sides and bottom of muffin cups. Bake crust at 325 degrees F for 6 minutes.

Cool crust. Fill with filling recipe above. A popsicle stick works great for spreading the filling in the mini muffin cups.

Oatmeal Pie

1 unbaked 9" pie shell
2 eggs
3/4 cup white corn syrup
1/2 cup butter, melted
1/2 cup sugar
1/2 cup brown sugar
3/4 cup oatmeal
1 cup evaporated milk
1 cup shredded coconut
1 teaspoon vanilla

Blend eggs, corn syrup, butter and sugars in a medium sized bowl for 3 minutes. Add oatmeal and evaporated milk; mix for 1 more minute. Add coconut and vanilla and blend well. Pour into pie shell. Bake at 350 degrees F for 30 to 40 minutes, until a knife inserted in the center comes out clean.

PIES AND MINI PIES: JOIN THE MINI PIE EXPLOSION

Oatmeal Mini Pies

** Use 2 9" crusts for 12 muffin cups or 24 mini muffin cups.

Spray muffin pans with Pam. Add a strip of parchment paper to each muffin cup to use as handles for removing the tiny pies easily. Fill with pie crust as directed below, depending on your mini pie size.

Make the Oatmeal Pie filling according to this recipe. Only fill muffin cups 3/4 full with pie filling. TOPS - Add lattice pastry strips, use tiny cookie cutters in pastry, top with pie crust (slit top for venting) or just leave the top open. Pinch the crusts together if topping with pie crust.

Mini pies bake a little faster than regular pies. Cook the mini oatmeal pies for about 15 to 20 minutes at 350 or 375 degrees F. If additional cooking time is needed, check the pies frequently until the crust is golden. Cool in pan.

Muffin/Cupcake Pan: 2-3/4" mini pies

Pie crust: Cut 3-1/2" or 4" circles with a biscuit cutter or use a bowl to cut the circle. Shape the pie crust into each muffin cup.

Mini Muffin Pan: 1-3/4" mini pies

Pie Crust: Make your favorite pie crust recipe. Roll the dough into 24 balls about 1" in diameter. Press the balls into the bottom and up sides of muffin cups.

Refrigerated Pie Crust: Cut 3" circles with a cookie cutter and shape into each muffin cup.

Peanut Butter Pie

Baked pie shell
1 cup powdered sugar
1/3 cup peanut butter
1 small box instant vanilla pudding
Whipped cream

Combine peanut butter and powdered sugar to form small crumbs. Reserve 1/4 cup of the crumbs, line baked pie shell with remaining crumbs. Prepare vanilla pudding according to package directions. Put pudding in pie shell. Top with whipped cream and sprinkle reserved crumbs on top.

PIES AND MINI PIES: JOIN THE MINI PIE EXPLOSION

Peanut Butter Mini Pies

** Use 2 9" crusts for 12 muffin cups or 24 mini muffin cups.
** Refrigerator pie crusts may be used.
** Add filling from peanut butter recipe after baking and cooling the mini pie crusts.

Spray muffin pans with Pam. Add a strip of parchment paper to the muffin cup to use as handles for removing the tiny pies easily. Fill muffin cups with pastry as directed below, depending on your mini pie size.

muffin pan recipe

Muffin/Cupcake Pan: 2-3/4" mini pies

Pie crust: Cut 3-1/2" or 4" circles with a biscuit cutter or use a bowl to cut the circle. Shape the pie crust into each regular size muffin cup. Bake at 450 degrees F for 8 to 10 minutes or until lightly browned.

mini muffin pan recipe

Mini Muffin Pan: 1-3/4" mini pies

Pie Crust: Make your favorite pie crust recipe. Roll the dough into 24 balls about 1" in diameter. Press the balls into the bottom and up sides of muffin cups. Bake at 400 degrees F 6 to 8 minutes or until lightly browned.

Refrigerated Pie Crust: Cut 3" circles using a round cutter and shape into each mini muffin cup or roll the dough into 24 balls about 1" in diameter. Press the balls into the bottom and up sides of mini muffin cups. Bake at 400 degrees F 6 to 8 minutes or until lightly browned.

Zucchini Pie

1 unbaked pie shell
6 cups zucchini, peeled, sliced and seeded
1 1/4 cups sugar
1 1/2 teaspoons cream of tartar
1 teaspoon cinnamon
1/8 teaspoon nutmeg
1/8 teaspoon salt

Combine all ingredients and place in a pie shell. Bake for 1 hour at 350 degrees F. Tastes like apple pie.

Zucchini Mini Pies

** Cut the zucchini into smaller bite-size pieces for mini pies.
** Use 2 9" crusts for 12 muffin cups or 24 mini muffin cups.

Spray muffin pans with Pam. Add a strip of parchment paper to each muffin cup to use as handles for removing the tiny pies easily. Fill with pie crust as directed below, depending on your mini pie size.

Make the Zucchini Pie filling according to this recipe. Only fill muffin cups 3/4 full with pie filling. TOPS - Add lattice pastry strips, use tiny cookie cutters in pastry, top with pie crust (slit top for venting) or just leave the top open. Pinch the crusts together if topping with pie crust.

Mini pies bake a little faster than regular pies. Cook the mini zucchini pies for about 15 to 20 minutes at 350 or 375 degrees F. If additional cooking time is needed, check the pies frequently until the crust is golden. Cool in pan.

muffin pan recipe

Muffin/Cupcake Pan: 2-3/4" mini pies

Pie crust: Cut 3-1/2" or 4" circles with a biscuit cutter or use a bowl to cut the circle. Shape the pie crust into each muffin cup.

mini muffin pan recipe

Mini Muffin Pan: 1-3/4" mini pies

Pie Crust: Make your favorite pie crust recipe. Roll the dough into 24 balls about 1" in diameter. Press the balls into the bottom and up sides of muffin cups.

Refrigerated Pie Crust: Cut 3" circles with a cookie cutter and shape into each muffin cup.

Mandarin Orange Pie

1 cup flour
1/2 teaspoon salt
3/4 cup sugar
1 teaspoon baking soda
1 11 oz. can mandarin oranges
1/2 cup brown sugar
1/2 cup chopped nuts

Mix together the flour, salt, sugar, baking soda and mandarin oranges with the juice from the can. Pour into a greased pie pan and top with 1/2 cup brown sugar and 1/2 cup chopped nuts. Bake at 325° F for 35 to 45 minutes. Serve warm or cold, with whipped cream or ice cream.

PIES AND MINI PIES: JOIN THE MINI PIE EXPLOSION

PIE CRUSTS

Pie Crusts

These pie crusts are never-fail recipes that don't require a cooking school certification to prepare. Don't worry if you don't have a rolling pin; you'll be able to use your fingers to press the dough into your pie pan for a time-saving crust that's sure to please.

Some of these recipes are prepared right in the pie plate, so cleanup is a snap. These recipes are perfect for impromptu gatherings and occasions when there just isn't enough time for a major baking session. You'll be amazed at how quickly you can prepare and serve a fresh-from-the-oven pie.

Pie Crust Tips

Just like many other abilities, good pie baking skill develops with experience and employing little tips and tricks you accumulate over the years. You may not be able to spend an afternoon baking with your county-fair-blue-ribbon-winning aunt or grandmother, but add a few of these time tested tips, and your pies will become ribbon worthy too.

Prepare Your Dough

Use ice water when making your pie dough. The shortening or butter needs to remain cold and the icy water helps keep it from melting.

Handle and mix the dough as little as possible. Overmixing will result in a tough crust.

Use a food processor to speed up mixing and minimize handling.

Chill your butter or shortening and cut into small chunks before blending with the flour.

Freeze your butter and shred with a cheese grater before blending with the flour.
After mixing your dough, divide it into two portions. The portion of the bottom crust should be a little larger than the top crust. Form into flattened balls, and cover with plastic wrap.

Allow the dough to rest for two hours in the refrigerator before rolling it out. After wrapping in plastic wrap, it can remain in the refrigerator for up to 24 hours. You can also freeze the dough at this point for up to two months.

Tenderize Your Pie Dough

Replace one teaspoon of water with lemon juice or vinegar for each cup of flour used in your dough recipe. This won't affect the flavor of your crust, but it keeps the gluten from forming strands that will make your crust tougher.

Rolling Out Your Dough

Rolling your dough on waxed paper makes life easy and clean up a breeze. Sprinkle a few drops of water on the counter, spread the moisture around with your hand, and place a sheet of wax paper over the wet area. Place your flattened ball of dough in the center and cover with a second sheet of paper.

Always roll from the center out when preparing a crust. Work equally around the circle, using firm, outward strokes. Keeping the perimeter as round and symmetrical as possible, work the dough in all directions.

A heavy rolling pin makes the job easier than a lightweight pin. A rolling pin with ball bearings rolls smoothly and easily. A marble rolling pin is a great investment if you bake a lot of pies.

Make the crust two inches larger in diameter than the pie plate.

Use the waxed paper to transfer the crust from the counter to the pan. Gently peel off the top piece of paper. Pick the crust up by the paper, fold in half and position over the pie pan with the paper on the top. Reposition the crust until it is centered, and allow it to settle into the pan. Carefully peel away the wax paper, and press the crust evenly into the pan. Use the same procedure for the top crust, and center it on top of the pie filling.

Use your kitchen scissors to cut away the excess crust after fitting it in the pie pan. You can also use the edge of a butter knife.

Use The Right Pie Pan

Don't use dark metal or shiny aluminum pans. The dark metal may cause the crust to brown too much. Shiny aluminum reflects heat, which may prevent the crust from browning. Use a glass or dull metal pie pan for best results.

Prevent Edges Of The Crust From Burning

Cover the rim of the pie after the first 15 minutes to ensure the edge does not burn. You can purchase aluminum pie crust shields at kitchen supply stores, or cut strips of aluminum to gently shape around the rim.

Vent Your Pie

Cut several vents in the top crust of your pie. This allows the steam to escape. This will keep the top crust from getting soggy.

Glaze The Crust

There are several things you can use to glaze your pie crust. It's certainly not necessary, but the glaze adds a beautiful finish to your pie that makes it a lovely presentation for your guests.

Use a very soft pastry brush to apply your glaze, and don't apply so much that you end up with puddles of the liquid.

Use milk or cream, and your pie will bake to a matte, reddish-brown color.
Beat a whole egg to glaze your pie crust. This will give a shiny, golden yellow finish to your pie.

Beat only the egg yolk for a deep, golden brown color. This glaze has a rich, high gloss finish.

Brush the crust with egg white mixed with a teaspoon of water. It doesn't change the color of the crust, but it gives the crust a sheen. You can also sprinkle a bit of sugar over the glaze before baking to give the pie a glittery appearance.

Prevent A Soggy Bottom Crust

If you are baking a single crust pie, brush it with egg white when it comes out of the oven. The egg will cook and seal the crust surface. Strained raspberry or apricot preserves, melted chocolate or clarified butter can be brushed over the surface of the crust. The coating solidifies and keeps the crust dry.

For a double crust, try baking your pie on a preheated baking stone or bake directly on the oven floor to help brown the bottom. This will help prevent a soggy crust.

Cool your pie on a wire rack. This allows the bottom to cool more rapidly and may prevent some sogginess.

Easy Pie Crust for Cream Pies

Put directly into pie pan:

1 1/2 teaspoons sugar
1 1/2 cups flour

Pour over the flour:

2 tablespoons milk
1/2 cup oil

Mix with a fork until well blended. Pat out with fingers into even covering. Bake at 425 degrees F for 12 to 15 minutes. Cool. Fill with any cream filling.

Mix and Press One-Crust Pastry

1 cup flour
1/2 teaspoon salt
1/4 cup shortening
2 teaspoons butter
1 teaspoon cold water

Place all ingredients in small mixing bowl and mix until particles are fine. (If mixture seems a little dry, add a few drops of water.) Press the crumb mixture evenly and firmly over the bottom and sides of a 9" pie pan with floured fingers. Flute the edges, if desired. Do not prick the crust. Bake at 425 degrees F for 12 to 15 minutes or fill and bake as desired.

Never Roll Pie Crust

1 1/2 cups flour
1 teaspoon salt
1 1/2 tablespoons sugar
1/2 cup salad oil
2 tablespoons milk

Sift together flour, salt and sugar in glass pie plate. Mix milk and oil together and pour into pie plate with dry ingredients. Mix all together with a fork. Pat with fingers to form a pie shell. Bake at 350 degrees F until brown.

Baked Cookie Crust

1 cup flour
3 tablespoons sugar
1/2 cup butter
1 egg yolk
1/2 teaspoon vanilla
1 teaspoon lemon juice
1/8 teaspoon salt

Combine flour, sugar, butter, egg yolk, vanilla, lemon juice and salt in a bowl. Blend with a pastry blender until a smooth ball forms. Cover and refrigerate for 1 hour. Roll out dough and place in 9-inch pie plate. Prick bottom of dough with fork. Bake shell in a 400 degree F oven for 7 minutes or until lightly browned. Cool.

For chocolate crust: Omit lemon juice and add 2 tablespoons unsweetened cocoa and 1 additional tablespoon sugar.

Lo-Cal Graham Cracker Crust

2/3 cup graham cracker crumbs
1/4 teaspoon unflavored gelatin
2 1/2 tablespoons diet margarine

Blend crumbs, margarine and gelatin in a small bowl with a fork. Spray a 9-inch pie plate with non-stick cooking spray. Press crumb moisture against the side and bottom of the plate. Bake crust in a 425 degrees F oven for 5 minutes or until lightly browned. Cool on wire rack.

Tarts

Party Mini Cheesecake Tarts

1 pound cream cheese, softened
1 teaspoon vanilla
2 large eggs
3/4 cup sugar
Cherry pie filling
Small vanilla wafers
Small foil cups (paper-lined)

Beat cream cheese, vanilla, eggs and sugar together. Place 1 vanilla wafer in paper-lined foil cups and fill 3/4 full with creamed mixture. Bake 10 minutes at 375 degrees F. When cool, top with small portion of cherry pie filling.

Pecan Tarts

1 cup chopped pecans
16 unbaked tart shells
1 cup sugar
4 eggs
1 cup light corn syrup
1/4 cup melted butter or margarine
1 teaspoon vanilla extract

Sprinkle the pecans into the tart shells. Mix the sugar and eggs in a medium bowl. Stir in the corn syrup, butter and vanilla. Spoon into the tart shells; place on a baking sheet. Bake at 350 degrees F for 30 to 40 minutes or until set.

Cherry Tarts

Crust:

3/4 cup graham cracker crumbs
2 tablespoons melted butter
1 tablespoon powdered sugar

Mix the crust ingredients together with a fork. Place equally in bottom of 12 cupcake paper liners and press firmly with bottom of a glass. Bake 10 minutes at 350 degrees F.

Filling:

8 ounce package cream cheese
1 egg
1 teaspoon vanilla
1/4 cup powdered sugar

Mix all together with mixer until smooth. Divide equally in the 12 cupcake liners. Cool in refrigerator. When cool, place canned cherry pie filling in each cup. Refrigerate overnight for best flavor.

Eggnog Custard Tarts

4 eggs
3 cups eggnog
1/2 cup sugar
1 teaspoon vanilla
1/4 teaspoon salt
2 tablespoons light rum
Ground nutmeg
4 1/2 inch tart pans

Make a double pie crust with one of our recipes or use the Pillsbury refrigerated pie crusts. Using just half of the pastry at a time, roll it out to 1/8 inch thickness. Cut out three 6 1/2 inch circles out of the pastry half. Line the pans with pastry. Flute or crimp the edge of the crust high and don't prick it. Do the same with the other pastry half. Bake in 450 degrees F oven for 5 minutes. Cool on rack.

For filling, in mixing bowl beat eggs slightly with rotary beater or fork. Stir in the eggnog, sugar, salt, vanilla and light rum; mix well. Places tart pans on cookie sheet. Pour some filling into each partially baked tart shell. Add a little nutmeg sprinkled on each tart. Bake in 350 degrees F oven about 40 minutes or till knife inserted in center comes out clean. Cool on rack. Cover; store in refrigerator.

Yield: 6 tarts

PIE TOPPINGS

Pie Toppings

Dry Up Your Weeping Meringues

To prevent your meringue pie from oozing liquid, you have several options for controlling the moisture. Try them all to see which works the best for you.

The meringue should be applied to a very hot filling. Do not allow the pie to cool before adding the topping.

Add a teaspoon of cornstarch to the sugar before adding it to your egg mixture when making your meringue.

Sprinkle very finely crushed cake crumbs over the filling before spreading the meringue.

Streusel Topping

1/4 cup flour
1/4 cup butter or margarine
1/4 cup sugar
1/4 cup dark brown sugar, packed
1 teaspoon cinnamon
1/4 teaspoon nutmeg

Combine the flour, butter, sugar, brown sugar, cinnamon and nutmeg in a bowl and mix well.

Yield: 1 cup

Easy Meringue

1/2 cup water
1 teaspoon cornstarch
1/8 teaspoon salt
1/4 cup sugar
3 egg whites

Combine water, cornstarch, salt and sugar. Cook over low heat until thickened. Cool. Beat 3 egg whites until they are very stiff. Fold whites into cooked mixture. Spread on pie and brown in 350 degrees F oven 12 to 15 minutes.

Meringue Topping

3 egg whites
6 teaspoons sugar

Beat egg whites in a mixing bowl until soft peaks form. Slowly add the sugar and beat until it forms stiff peaks and the sugar dissolves. Spread over hot filling.

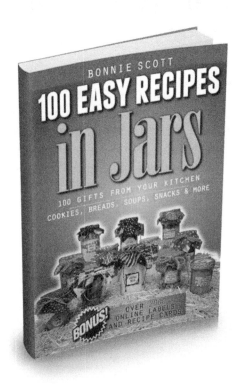

100 Easy Recipes In Jars

Now in Paperback and Kindle versions

Other Books by Bonnie Scott

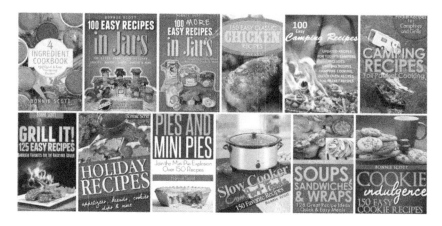

Camping Recipes: Foil Packet Cooking
100 Easy Camping Recipes
4 Ingredient Cookbook
Slow Cooker Comfort Foods
Bacon Cookbook: 150 Easy Bacon Recipes
150 Easy Classic Chicken Recipes

Grill It! 125 Easy Recipes
Soups, Sandwiches and Wraps
Simply Fleece
Fish & Game Cookbook
Cookie Indulgence: 150 Easy Cookie Recipes
Pies and Mini Pies
Holiday Recipes: 150 Easy Gifts from Your Kitchen

IN JARS
100 Easy Recipes in Jars
100 More Easy Recipes in Jars
Desserts in Jars

All titles available in Paperback and Kindle versions at Amazon.com

BONNIE SCOTT

Made in the USA
Las Vegas, NV
09 November 2024